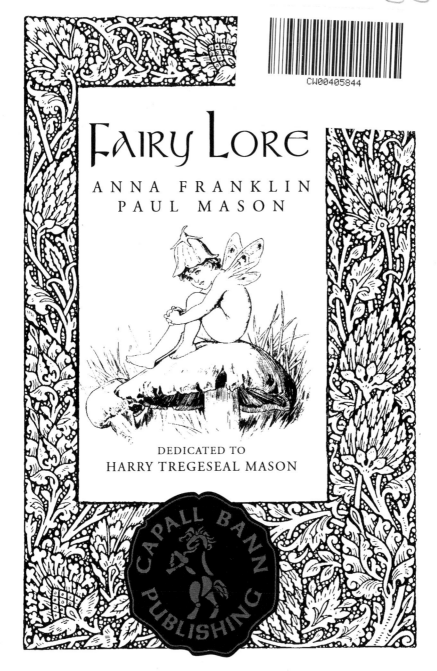

Fairy Lore

ANNA FRANKLIN
PAUL MASON

DEDICATED TO
HARRY TREGESEAL MASON

CAPALL BANN PUBLISHING

Fairy Lore

Published by Capall Bann Publishing
Freshfields
Chieveley
Berkshire
RG20 8TF

CONTENTS

PART ONE- FAIRY LORE   1
What do Fairies Look Like?   6
Seeing Fairies   11
Fairy Realms   15
    Avalon   19
    Channel Isles   19
    Emain Ablach   20
    Hy-Breasail   20
    Isle of Man   20
    Isles of the Blest or the Fortunate Islands   21
    Lochlann (or Sorcha)   22
    Gwerddonau Llion   22
    Tir Nan Og (The Land of Youth) 22
    Ynis Gwydrin (The Isle of Glass)   23
Fairy Food   25
Elf Bolts and Other Fairy Ills   29
Protection Against Fairies   35
    Clothes   37
    Iron   37
    Christian Symbols   38
    Pagan Symbols   38
    Bells   39
    Oatmeal   39
    Mirrors   39
    Baking   40
    Plants   40
    Fire   42
    Urine   42
    Water   42

Fairy Plants   43
    Elder   44
    Foxglove   45
    Reed   45
    Fly Agaric   46
    Fairy Ring Mushroom   47
    Hazel   47
    Wild Thyme   48
    Heather   48
    Ragwort   50
    Silverweed   50
    Alder   50
    Bluebell   50
    Primrose   51
    Cowslips   52
    Four-leafed Clover   52
    Hawthorn   52
    Fern   53
    Rowan   53
    Oak   54
    Birch   54
    Blackthorn   55
    Blackberry   56
    Apple   56
    Fungi   57
Fairy Animals   59
    Butterfly   60
    Cat   60
    Cattle   61
    Boar   63
    Cuckoo   65
    Deer   65

Dog 66
Snail 67
Frog 68
Pig 68
Horse 69
Bat 70
Goat 71
Eagle 72
Woodpecker 73
Salmon 73
Hare 74
Changelings 75
The Sure Signs of a Changeling 77
Making a Changeling Reveal its Nature 77
Returned Children 79
How to Stop Fairies Kidnapping a Child 81
Fairy Abductions 83
Fairy Loves 87
The Test of Love 89
The Lay D'Ywenec 90
Aine 92
Melusina 93
Penelop 94
The Fairy of Llyn y Fan Fach 95
Visits to Fairyland 97
Tam Lin 99
Thomas the Rhymer 100
Fairy Music 101
Fairy Gifts 107
Fairy Days and Festivals 115
Friday 116
Wednesday 116

The Vernal Equinox   117
Beltane   117
Midsummer   118
Lughnasa   118
The Autumn Equinox   119
Samhain (Halloweeen)   119
The Winter Solstice (Yule)   120
Fairies and Witches   121

PART TWO- WHAT ARE FAIRIES?   125
Fallen Angels   129
A Seperate Race   133
The Cult of the Dead   137
Natue Spirits   143
The Old Gods   151
Elementals, Earthlights and UFOs   157
      Elementals   158
      Earthlights   159
      UFOs   161
Hallucinations and the Shamanic Experience   163

INDEX   170

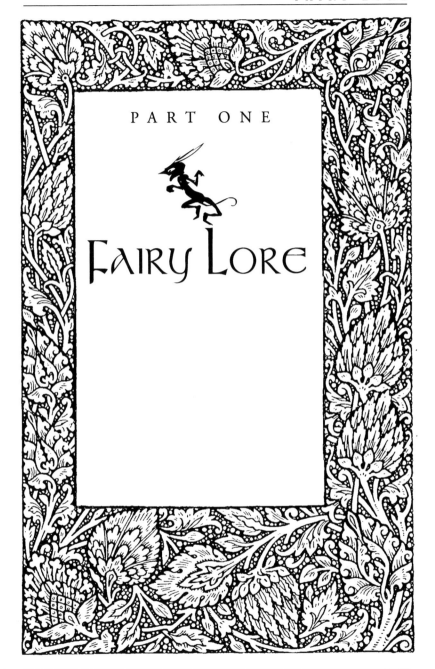

PART ONE

FAIRY LORE

Fairies are
mysterious creatures
sometimes seen in
wild and lonely places

There are legends of fairies all over the world, mysterious creatures who live apart from the race of mankind but who are sometimes seen in wild and lonely places. Some are large and some are small, some are good and some are evil. Many are solitary beings living alone to guard a well, a hill, a tree or a lake. Some aristocratic fairies gather together in large bands to form a fairy court.

The world of the fairy sometimes impinges on that of mankind. Their kingdoms appear and disappear. Usually fairies are only seen in the blinking of an eye, though there are tales of humans who have spent extended periods with them, or feasting and dancing with them for what seems to be a night, only to find that many years have passed in the human world. Human men and women have occasionally become the lovers of a fairy, but this relationship always has conditions and taboos imposed on it, and should the fairy lover leave for any reason- usually because of the breaking of a taboo- then the human will pine away and die.

The English word 'fairy' or 'faerie' is derived, by way of the French fé, from the Latin *fatare* meaning 'to enchant'. Variations on the spelling include fayerye, fairye, fayre and faery. In England, Geoffrey Chaucer made the words fairy and elf interchangeable, though the word 'elf' is from the Scandinavian *alfar*, a term that relates to mountains and water. The Welsh call fairies *Tylwyth Teg* meaning 'Fair Family'. In Scotland they are the *Daoine Coire* or 'Honest Folk' or *Daoine Beaga* 'Little Folk' and to the Irish *Daoine Matha*, 'Good People' or *Daoine Sidhe*, meaning' People of the Hills'. *Sidhe* simply means 'hill', referring to the hollow hills and mounds where fairies are said to live, though it has been suggested that it may be from the same etymological root as the Hindustani word *siddhi* meaning 'something which controls the elements'.

However, in the past it was considered unlucky to name the fairies, or even to use the word 'fairy' perhaps because to do so may have summoned them, or because using a name without its owner's permission was a threat or challenge. It was wise to call them 'the Good People', 'the Little People', 'the Gentry', 'the Mother's Blessing', 'Good Neighbours', 'Wee Folk' or 'the Hidden People', just as the ancient Greeks called the Furies, the terrifying goddesses of vengeance, 'The Kindly Ones'. Talking about fairies was to invite disasters, the least of which was being struck by blindness.

Fairies are generally thought to be immortal, though some say that they are merely long-lived, existing for between 400 and 1000 years. William Blake witnessed a fairy funeral in his garden, with the corpse borne on a rose leaf. It was buried with ceremony and chants before the fairies disappeared. Perhaps though, fairy funerals are only pantomimes in imitation of human beings.

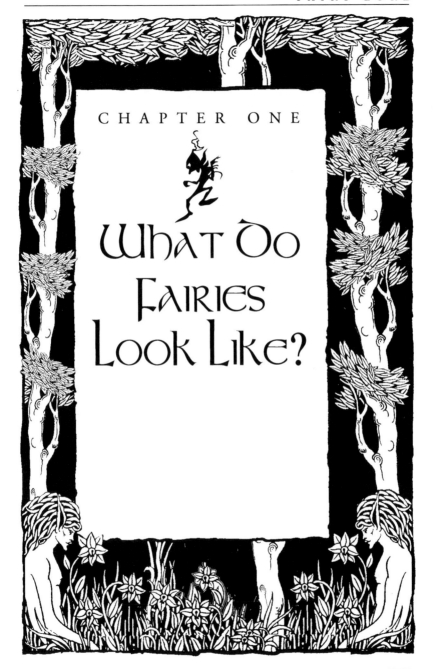

CHAPTER ONE

What Do Fairies Look Like?

The sentimental late Victorian view of fairies was that they were all delicate, miniature, butterfly winged creatures but older accounts described them as being human size or larger and often ugly. They usually appear in human form, but since they can exert a glamour that deceives the eye and make a crone seem to be a young girl or a rough cottage a palace, it is impossible to know their true appearance. However, there are always signs to betray a fairy origin, like webfeet, feet back to front, goat's hoofs, squint eyes, pointed ears or cow's tails. Some fairy women have a frightful front tooth, or very long breasts. In Mull fairies only have one nostril. The Irish banshee gives herself away by devouring a whole cow at a single meal. Many fairies are also expert shapeshifters and can choose to appear in a variety of non-human forms such as fire, moss, deer, birds and other animals. Fairy spotters say the beings sometimes appear to radiate a shimmering light, or to have a musky odour.

It is said that as humans spread over the landscape and as farms, villages and towns appeared the fairies retreated further and further into the wilder places, perhaps eventually disappearing altogether, going into the west. Some believe that as time passed they shrank in size from human or larger to become very small. In a Cornish story of the nineteenth century a greedy old man tried to steal some fairies' treasure as they feasted on the Gump, a hill outside St. Just. The fairies were so tiny he could cover the whole fairy feast with his hat, but as he raised it to trap them a shrill whistle was heard and his hand became fixed in the air and all went dark around him.

Many British fairies are described as being the size of young children. Writing in 1705 John Beaumont described an experience with fairies:

'...the two that constantly attended myself appeared both in Women's Habit, they being of a Brown complexion, and about Three Foot in Stature; they had both black, loose Network Gowns, tyed with a black Sash about their Middles, and within the Network appear'd a Gown of Golden Colour, with somewhat of a Light striking thro' it...they had white Linen Caps on, with Lace on them, about three Fingers breadth.'

In 1911 T.C.Kermode described an encounter with the Isle of Man fairies:

'...I saw come in twos and threes a great crowd of little beings smaller than Tom Thumb and his wife. All of them, who appeared like soldiers, were dressed in red. They moved back and forth amid the circle of light, as they formed into order like troops drilling.'

The earth fairies that dwell beneath the ancient mounds are usually small and look like beautiful humans. They love music and dancing and live luxuriously in their underground palaces. According to Irish lore the fairy king and princes dress in green with red caps bound with a golden fillet. The queen and court ladies are robed in silver gauze, spangled diamonds and their long golden hair sweeps the ground. In Ireland all the trooping fairies wear green jackets and the solitary ones red. On the western coast the red jacket is covered by a frieze one, and in Ulster the solitary fairy wears a cocked hat.

In Skye the fairy women are dressed in green, while the males are called 'little red men' [*daoine beaga ruadh*] as their clothes are dyed with lichen. The women's coats are shaggy, and their caps wrinkled. The men sometimes have blue bonnets. In Orkney fairies are all considered ugly and evil, and a Shetland writer described the local faries as short with small faces, yellow complexions, red eyes and green teeth. They dress in dark grey and wear brown wool mittens. Welsh fairies customarily dress in red and white.

Some fairies can fly, though few have wings. Usually they ride on ragwort stalks, or by wearing magic caps or by reciting spells. Most of them can appear or disappear at will.

In mediaeval lore the fairies came to be divided into the aristocracy, who

appeared in groups, and the common fairies, who appeared individually. The common fairies were elusive and often the only sign of their existence was in their passing, with the bending of the flowers or the rustling of the leaves in the branches, or the patterns of Jack Frost in the windowpane. They were the guardians of individual streams, trees, forests, pools and streams, or sometimes of private houses and particular families.

The aristocrats were called Heroic or Trooping Fairies and belonged to the Seelie Courts of Scotland or the Daoine Sidhe [pronounced Theena Shee] of Ireland. The Daoine Sidhe were believed to be the diminished remnants of the Tuatha de Danann ['People of the Goddess Dana'], who may have been legendary gods or an actual race who were driven underground by the Celtic Milesian invaders. The Danaan were thought to have taken four gifts to Ireland- the spear, the sword, the cauldron and the stone, representing the four elements and the power of the elemental kingdoms.

In the Middle Ages fairy aristocrats were thought to be human sized and very beautiful. They passed their time hunting, hawking, and feasting. Tales are told of the Fairy Rade [ride] when they rode in procession behind their king and queen on white horses hung with silver bells. These types of fairies are more common in

Scotland than either England or Wales. One description comes from an old woman of Dumfriesshire in the early 1800s:

'A leam of light was dancing over them, more bonnie than moonshine. They were wee, wee folks with green scarves on. They rode on braw wee white nags with uncommonly long swooping tails and manes hung with whistles that the wind played on. This and their tongues when they sang was like the sound of a far away psalm.'

The last Fairy Rade was witnessed at the beginning of the nineteenth century by a herdboy and his sister at a hamlet near Glen Eathie. A procession of dwarfish strangers rode by and the boy asked them who they were and where they were going. The leader replied:

'Not of the race of Adam. The people of peace shall never more be seen in Scotland.'

CHAPTER
TWO

SEEING FAIRIES

Fairies can become visible or invisible at will, or be visible to one person while being invisible to another, though sometimes they can be spied at their revels unawares. Fairy kingdoms are supposed to exist in another dimension to that of humankind, though they sometimes appear for a brief instant to mortal eyes. There is a square of turf in Wales where, if you trip over it, you will get a single glimpse of fairies, though the spot can never be found twice.

Not everyone can see fairies; people born in the morning cannot see spirits or the fairy world, while those born at night have power over ghosts and can see both fairies and the spirits of the dead.

People who have fairy blood themselves possess the gift of second sight and can perceive what others do not. Young girls just prior to puberty are more likely to be able to see fairies than adults.

A person whose eyes have been touched with fairy water or the application of a magic ointment can see them when they are present. The sight can be opened by a four-leaf clover, as the milkmaid who accidentally picked a four-leaf clover with the grass she used to soften the weight of the pail on her head discovered. When next she looked at her cow she saw dozens of fairies milking it.

An old recipe to make a potion to enable you to see fairies ran thus:

'Take a pint of Sallet oil and put it in a glasse, first washing it with rose water. Then put thereto the budds of hollyhocke, of marygolde, of young hazle and the topps of wild thyme. Take the grasse of a fairy throne; then all these put into the glasse...dissolve three dayes in the sunne, and keep it for thy use.'

You must gaze steadily to see fairies- if you blink they will disappear. They are most often seen at noon, midnight or twilight. They are also sometimes seen on wild stormy nights of driving mist and rain. Traditionally the best times to see fairies are Halloween, May Day, Midsummer Day, Lady Day and Christmas Day [the old Celtic festivals of Samhain, Beltane, The Midsummer Solstice, The Vernal Equinox, and the Midwinter Solstice]. On these nights the fairy dwellings open and they may be seen feasting inside.

Fairies also appear when spoken of and when a desire is expressed for their assistance, when proper precautions are omitted or when those vulnerable to fairy attentions, such as newborn babies, are neglected.

Fairies are often said to live beneath the ancient burial mounds,
the Hollow Hills of lore.
Entrance to burial chamber at Newgrange, Co Meath, Ireland.

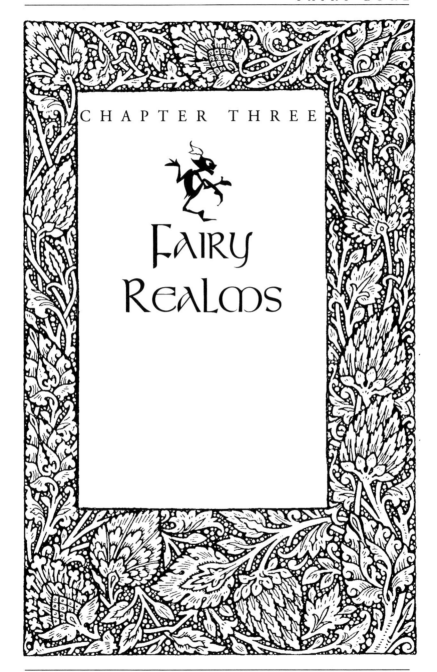

CHAPTER THREE

Fairy
Realms

F airies are often said to live beneath the ancient burial
mounds, the Hollow Hills of lore, where they feast and
dance. Sometimes at night these hills are said to sparkle
with light and if you press an ear to the hill you will hear their
revels. If a person sleeps on the mound fairy music will enter their
soul and they will never be the same again.

There are stories from the Western Isles that recount incidences
of people tethering horses or cows to mounds only to have a head
appear out of the earth telling them to tether it somewhere else as
it lets rain into the house, or that the tether pin has nearly been
driven into one of the inmates. Fairies are grateful to any farmer
who keeps the mound clean from horse droppings and does not
disturb it with a tether pin or spade. They reward him by driving
his cattle to the shelter of the mound on stormy nights.

The hills are used to hide gold and bury fairy kings- King Sil is
said to sit in his golden armour on his horse inside Silbury Hill in
Wiltshire. Underneath the lakes and in the heart of the hills the
fairies have palaces of pearl and gold. They are served on vessels of
gold and each fairy chief wears a circlet of gold around his head,
according to the Irish. Fairies are very numerous, more numerous

than the human race, and hide much treasure in their palaces. All the treasure of wrecked ships is theirs, and all the gold that men have buried in the earth when they were in danger and never retrieved. All the gold of the mines and all the jewels in the rocks belong to them and in the Sifra or fairy house the walls are of silver and the pavement gold, the banquet hall is lit by the glimmer of diamonds. Anyone digging into the fairy mounds to steal the gold will be warned by strange voices, sounds and storms and should take heed, or disaster and even death will follow. A Trow warned an Orkney farmer not to interfere with a mound in his field on pain of losing six cows and six funerals from his house. The farmer ignored the warning and suffered the penalty.

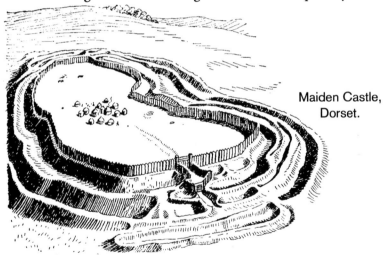

Maiden Castle, Dorset.

Earthworks or forts [sometimes called raths or liss] are also associated with fairies. It is said that when the ancient race moved out the fairies moved in. They are sacred to the Fair Folk and no tree on them should be cut down, nor should anything be built on them. If a man should be rash enough to attempt either sacrilege the fairies will blast his eyes or give him a crooked mouth. In the 1970s Irish workers refused to destroy a rath to expand the runways of Shannon airport and the plans had to be amended.

In Scots Gaelic the name *sithein* [pronounced shi-en] is given to any place the fairies take up residence. The *tolman* is a small green knoll or hummock, *bac* a bank of sand or earth, *cnoc* [knock or knowe] a little knoll, dun a rocky mound, *othan* a green elevation in wet ground. Sometimes a single family, sometimes a whole community, tenants these dwellings.

Near Logan Rock in Cornwall there are sheltered places between the rocks with ferns and sea pinks, which are said to be fairy gardens. St Levan said:

'When I have been to sea close under the cliffs, of a fine summer's night, I have heard the sweetest music, and seen hundreds of little lights moving about amongst what looked like flowers. Ay! And they are flowers too, for you may smell the sweet scent far out at sea. Indeed, I have heard many of the old men say that they have smelt the sweet perfume and heard the fairy music from the fairy gardens of the castle when more than a mile from the shore.'

It is said that you can see only see pinks by day, but those who have seen the gardens in the midsummer moonlight say they are covered with flowers of every colour, all more brilliant than any mortal flower.

To find the entrance to a fairy hill you should walk round it nine times around it at the full moon. Certain nights are best for this exercise and the mounds are supposed to open at Halloween [the old festival of Samhain] and you might get a glimpse inside. Sometimes a procession of lights can be seen moving from one hill to another, especially at Lammas [2nd August, the old Celtic festival of Lughnasa]. At Hollantide [11th November- old Samhain] the Hillmen or Hogmen, the most feared of the Manx fairies, move their abode, and one should not venture out then. They use well-trodden paths running in straight lines between the mounds. Any building on one of these fairy ways will meet with disturbances.

In addition there are several legendary fairy isles and kingdoms including:

Avalon

In British legend, this is the magical island outside time and space where illness, old age and death are unknown. The island is covered in apple orchards [the name means 'Isle of Apples'] and inhabited by nine sisters of which Morgan Le Fay is the most beautiful and most powerful. She has knowledge of shapeshifting and can turn herself into any animal or bird, and knows the properties of all plants for healing and magic. The fifteenth century poet Lydgate described Arthur as 'a king crowned in the land of the fairy' and says that he was taken by four fairy queens to Avalon, where he still lies with his knights under a fairy hill until Britain shall need him again. Some associate Avalon with modern day Glastonbury.

Channel Isles

The Channel Isles were once thought to be fairy islands, perhaps because of the many prehistoric graves, stone circles and monuments there. Locals believed that they had been built by *Les Petits Faótiaux* [the fairies] to live in. The prehistoric sites themselves were sometimes called *pouquelaie* or 'goblin's path'.

Fairies once invaded Guernsey. A girl called Michelle de Garis fell in love with a beautiful, tiny man she found beneath a hedge. He was one of the Secret People of England and they sailed away together, leaving as a gift for Michelle's parents a bulb, which blossomed into the lovely Guernsey Lily. After a while more fairies arrived from England, all demanding brides like Michelle. The islanders refused to give up their women and tried to fight off the fairies, but lost the battle. The fairies married local women and this is why most islanders are short. The few tall people of the island are descended from the two human men who survived the battle.

Emain Ablach

In one Celtic legend the sea god Manannan summoned the hero Bran and his followers to the Isle of Emain Ablach [the Isle of Women] which was supported on four bronze pillars and solely inhabited by women. There they were entertained royally, but after a year they decided they would like to see Ireland once again. As they left, the women made them promise not to set foot on land. Eventually, the ship sighted Ireland and the adventurers shouted news of their exploits ashore. The incredulous inhabitants replied that Bran and his ship were only an ancient legend. At this, one of the sailors was so disturbed that he determined to wade ashore and find out what was going on, but as soon as his feet touched the land, he crumbled to dust. The crew realised that they could never return home after being in the realms of the fairy, and sailed away, never to be seen again.

Hy-Breasail

According to the Irish this fairy island lies in the west and only appears once every seven years. It once had to stay put when a red-hot arrow was fired into it. Many have tried to find Hy Breasail and maps have even existed, which usually depicted it as round, divided in the centre by a river, leading to comparisons with Atlantis.

Isle of Man

This very real island in the Irish Sea was thought to be a fairy domain. It is named after the Celtic sea god Manannan and is said to have been created when the giant Fin MacCool who scooped out a chunk of Irish land and thrust it into the Irish Sea. The hole that was left became Lough Neagh. The dense mists that often envelop the island are said to be the result of a mermaid's curse: she punished the whole island when a youth rejected her advances.

The island is steeped in fairy lore and the inhabitants say that if you put your ear to the Dalby Mountain you can hear the fairies or *Sheean-ny-Feaynid* ['sound of the infinite']. No islander would cross the Ballona Bridge [Fairy Bridge] without offering their greetings to the little folk beneath.

Fairies are said to be rarer in the Isle of Man since the coming of the railways, objecting to the iron which is death to them. Isle of Man fairies vary in size from that of human children, to smaller, deformed beings. They dress in green, usually have large ears and steal horses at night to hunt with fairy hounds They are easily offended, as a drunken farmer discovered when he swore at a group of them. The next day his horse and all his cattle died, and forty days later he was dead too. Islanders learned to protect themselves from the attentions of fairies with iron, salt, the bible, yellow flowers and rowan twigs.

Isles of the Blest or the Fortunate Islands
These fairy islands are only seen in the mist along the red path of light from the setting sun viewed from the western coast of Ireland.

Lochlann (or Sorcha)

An underwater fairy kingdom off the coast of Scotland.

Gwerddonau Llion (The Green Meadows of Enchantment)

Sailors occasionally glimpse The Green Meadows of Enchantment, a fairy land beneath the waves somewhere in the Bristol Channel between Somerset and Pembrokeshire. The islands are rarely visible, and are only seen by accident. During the nineteenth century some sailors landed on the islands and joined the fairies in their revels, but when they sailed away and looked back, the islands had vanished. In the fifth century the British King Gavran made a voyage in search of these islands, but whether he ever found them is not known, since he was never seen again. He may be there still, feasting with the fairies.

Fairies from the islands are reputed to have once regularly visited the markets of Milford Haven and Laugharne, silently making their purchases and always leaving the right money. The people of Milford Haven had a special ability to see the fairy islands and knew that the fairies went to and fro via a subterranean tunnel under the sea.

Some claimed that the island fairies were really certain druids, who could not enter heaven because they were Pagans, but not bad enough to enter hell

Tir Nan Og (The Land of Youth)

It is always spring here, and there is no ageing, illness or death, or even work as there is always fruit on the trees. When the Tuatha de Danaan fled from the physical realm of Ireland they went to Tir Nan Og where they live feasting, hunting, lovemaking and playing music. They can indulge in their love of fighting with impunity, as anyone killed will rise again the next day.

Oisin [pronounced Isheen] was the son of Finn, chief of the Fenian warriors of Ireland. He was hunting one day when Niamh of the Golden Hair, daughter of the god Manannan, approached him. She had chosen him for her lover and together they journeyed to Tir Nan Og. After three hundred years he expressed a wish to see his home and she lent him a fairy horse, with the caution not to let his feet touch the earth. He was dismayed to see that all had changed, and St Patrick had converted Ireland to Christianity. Even the men seemed feebler. He saw three trying to move a rock and as he lent down to give them a hand his saddle girth suddenly snapped and he fell to the earth. The horse vanished and he became ancient and blind. St Patrick found him and tried to convert him to Christianity, but Oisin could not see the point of an afterlife where there was no feasting, hunting or loving beautiful women and preferred to stay a Pagan.

Ynis Gwydrin (The Isle of Glass)

A fairy island off the coast of Wales with crystal palaces.

These fairy islands are always difficult to get to. Some are only seen in certain conditions, while some float and others are usually submerged. King Arthur, voyaging in his ship Prydwen visited many such islands, as did the Irish saint Brendan. One thing is certain; if any iron or steel is brought onto one of these islands they must stay put and cannot disappear or sink beneath the waves.

Strict protocols must be followed when visiting a fairy island, however. Every New Year's morning a door opened in a rock by a Welsh lake where a secret passage led to an island in the middle of the water. Visitors would be welcomed, feasted and feted in lovely gardens, but warned that the island was a secret and nothing should be removed from it. One day a visitor stole a flower, thinking it would be lucky. The moment he returned to the mortal realms, the flower vanished and he fell down unconscious. Since that day the door has remained closed.

CHAPTER FOUR

Fairy Food

F airies are said to sip nectar from flowers and to love honey and milk. In Cornwall, any milk spilt by accident was regarded as a gift to the fairies. One early writer said that they lived on a diet of milk and saffron and ate neither flesh nor fish. They also eat the root of the silverweed which is turned up by the plough in spring, the stalks of heather, the milk of red deer and goats and barleymeal.

Others say that fairy food consists of ordinary food from which they have taken the *toradh* [the substance or benefit] leaving only the semblance. Those humans who eat fairy food are as hungry afterwards as before.

Mortals who return from the land of the fairy often pine away and die, though people rescued from fairyland rarely suffer the same kind of longing that affects those who willingly share the fairy feasts and dancing. If you find yourself among the fairies you should not eat the fairy food as this will bind you to stay with the fairies forever. This is reminiscent of the Greek myth of the Goddess of Spring Persephone, who was forced to spend six months of every year in the underworld because she ate six seeds of a pomegranate there.

Fairy food is not always what it seems. Sometimes if grace is said over the victuals, they turn out to be horsedung. A goblet of mead may reveal itself to be an acorn filled with brackish water or a seeming royal banquet nothing but faded autumn leaves. In Innisboffin it is said that if anyone is unlucky enough to hear the fairy music or drink the fairy wine, they will be dead before the year is out.

One Irish tale of a fairy feast concerns a young man who fell asleep in a hayrick. When he awoke he found himself in a great hall where little men were at work; spinning, weaving and making elf bolts, while pipers played them tunes.

As he watched in puzzlement an old man approached him and told him to make himself useful as people were expected for dinner. He led the way to a kitchen where an old woman was hanging up on a meat hook. He told the astonished boy that she 'was dinner'. He instructed the young man to cut her up and boil her. Shocked, the young man fell down speechless but the old man said that it wouldn't hurt her, she was a miser in the world above, both cruel and bitter.

'Now,' he explained, 'we have her and her soul will never rest in peace, because her body will be cut into bits and the soul will wander looking for it.'

The young man then found himself in a beautiful hall where a sumptuous banquet was laid, the table groaning with delicious looking chickens, butter, cakes and pastries. There were sparkling crystal goblets of wine. The fairy prince welcomed him and invited him to sit down and eat. The young man, thinking of what he had seen in the kitchen, cleverly replied that as no priest had blessed the food he couldn't eat it.

'At least have some wine,' urged the prince. As the boy was very thirsty he seized the cup and quaffed the blood red liquid; it was the most delicious drink he had ever tasted. As he put down the glass the building shook, the lights went out and he found himself back in the hayrick.

The fairy wine burned in his veins for the remainder of his life. A restless longing to return to the fairy mansion haunted him, and eventually he pined away and died in sadness.

Any food left outside the house after sundown becomes the property of the fairies and is unfit for either humans or animals. Any crops left in the fields after Halloween either becomes the property of the fairies, or certain wicked fairies, like the phooka, will blight them.

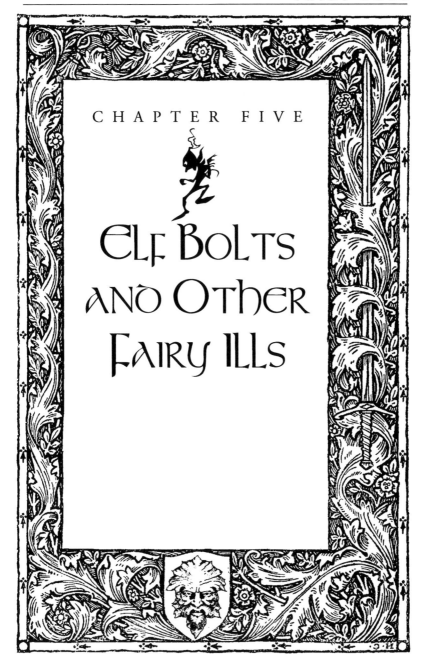

CHAPTER FIVE

Elf Bolts and Other Fairy Ills

The small flint arrowheads, made by stone age man, were once thought to have been manufactured by fairies and were called elf-bolts, 'elf-arrows' or 'elf-shot'. The elves and fairies were thought to use them to cause harm, propelling them into humans or livestock. Isobel Gowdie, the Scottish witch, said

'...as for elf arrows-heads the devil shapes them with his own hand and so delivers them to the elf boys'.

Deaths were attributed to them and it was thought they could induce paralysis; the origin of the word 'stroke' for paralysis is derived from 'elf-stroke'.

If a cow was suspected of being elf shot then it was usually necessary to send for a wise woman who would examine the cow for hairless patches or lumps under the skin. She would proceed to pierce the spot with a needle and if the cow did not bleed the diagnosis was confirmed. Every wise woman had her own remedies but some of these might include firing guns over the cow, whispering in its ears or giving it drinks off silver platters. One wise woman used pelleted verses torn from the bible.

Humans were also liable to elf shot, like the man sent lame for ploughing a trow hill. The fairy flint [*spor sith*] was frequently shot at the hunter because he killed the hinds the fairies needed for their milk.

Fairy darts were often aimed at the fingers, causing the joints to swell and go red and inflamed. An eminent 'fairy doctor' [a wise woman who specialised in curing fairy ills] made the cure of fairy darts her speciality and was sent for all round Ireland. She had no power unless she was asked to cure, and she took no reward until the dart was extracted and the cure effected. The treatment included a salve, the ingredients of which she kept secret.

In Scottish tradition elves could not throw the bolts themselves, but must compel some mortal whom they were carrying about to do so. If the victim was a friend then the thrower could usually manage to miss and the bolt would be found lying harmlessly beside the intended victim.

If you can find an elf bolt it is a lucky charm and will guard against any further attacks by elf-bolts. It can also cure wounds when rubbed on them. You should never give an elf bolt away, however, as this will be an invitation for the fairies to kidnap you.

There are other fairy objects which are lucky charms if they are found. A substance called 'elf's blood' [*fuil siochaire*] may be found on the shores of the Hebrides. It looks like a holed stone and is half red and half black. The fairy spade [*caibe sith*] is a smooth slippery black stone shaped like the sole of a shoe. It can be put in

water which will then cure sick people and cattle. The small, round fossil called an echinite is known as a Fairy Loaf.

In addition there are several other ills and mischiefs caused by fairy attentions:

- In Norway people fear the elf wind or *alvgest* which is the breath of elves and which covers the body of a person with blisters. To cure it the bible must be opened and the pages brushed over the body several times.
- Paralysis is often caused by the invisible presence of a fairy market
- Cramps are a punishment for annoying the fairies
- Tuberculosis is caused by eating fairy food or by visiting a fairy hill at night
- Impetigo and lice
- Infantile paralysis indicates that the baby is a changeling
- Rheumatism, cramps and bruising
- Childhood deformities - if a child is left alone the fairies will appear and give its limbs a twist.
- Elf locks [tangles in the hair or horses' manes]
- English fairies can steal your shadow, which will eventually cause you to fade away and die. However, if you can manage to steal a fairy's shadow he or she must grant you a wish.

Fairies are known to be thieves, but when they take something they take only its substance or spirit, so when a cow is elf-taken it appears to be struck down by some disease. It will lie down and refuse to get up. Though it will continue to eat, it will produce no milk. When it dies its flesh will turn out to be a stock of alder wood or some rubbish.

Fairies can also steal the spirit of the land itself. When this happens the fields appear to yield a crop but the ears of corn will not fill out, the harvest will be slender and the animal fodder without nourishment.

Fairies can only take away what selfish humans deserve to lose. If you 'over look a child' [i.e. look on it with envy] then the fairies have it in their power. When people become miserly and refuse to share their possessions or do not value them them the fairies will take the goodness out of them. When a farmer grumbles about his crop, even if it is good, the fairies will take the substance out of it. When you mislay something and can't find it, no matter how hard you look, it is almost certain that the fairies have taken it.

There evry herd, by sad experience, knows
How, wing'd with fate, their elf-shot arrows fly;
When the sick ewe her summer food foregoes,
Or, stretch'd on earth, the heart-smit heifers lie.
Willial Collins
'An Ode on the Popular Superstitions of the Highlands of Scotland'

Go not to the hills of Erin
When the night winds are about;
Put up your bar and shutter
And so keep the danger out.

For the good-folk whirl within it,
And they pull you by the hand,
And they push you on the shoulder,
Till you move to their command.

And lo! you have forgotten
What you have known of tears,
And you will not remember
That the world goes full of years:

A year there is a lifetime
And a second but a day;
And an older world will meet you
Each morn you come away.
Dora Sigerson, 'The Wind on the Hills'

CHAPTER SIX

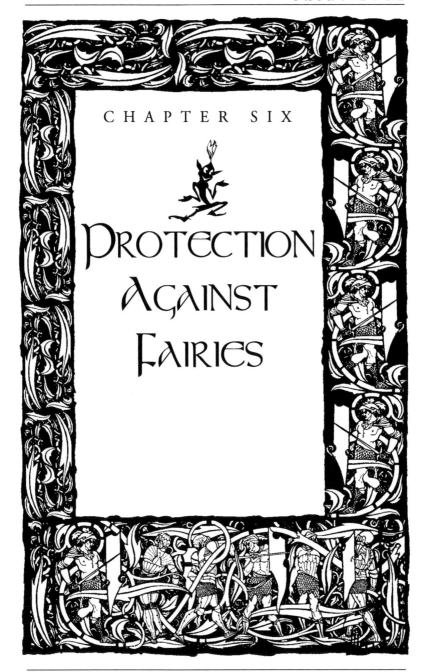

PROTECTION AGAINST FAIRIES

U nless careful precautions are taken, fairies will gain entrance to your property by a variety of methods, where they will delight in causing untold damage.

They can gain admission into homes by means of the last of the baking, called the *fallaid bannock*, unless a hole is put into it, a piece broken off, or a red hot coal placed on top of it. They can also enter by means of the water in which men's feet have been washed, which they will splash about in. Unless the fire has been properly raked and banked up to keep it alive for the night the fairies will come down the chimney.

In Ireland, fairies gain access to houses thus: one of them ascends to the keyhole, carrying a thread and on it descends to the inside, where he fastens it to some article of furniture. Then the fairies march along it to the parlour or pantry, first the piper, playing a fairy march, followed by the others.

If the band of the spinning wheel is left stretched on the wheel, particularly on Saturday evenings, fairies will come in and undo all your work. Eggshells are a favourite retreat of fairies, therefore the shell should always be broken after use to prevent the fairies taking up residence. Water should be taken into the house at night, because if there is nothing for the fairies to drink they will suck a sleeper's blood. Husbands and wives should go to bed at the same time- if the wife stays up later than her husband she is liable to be abducted by fairies.

To protect against the attentions of fairies there are several effective methods:

Clothes
If fairies are troubling you or if you are being pixie-led on a journey, turn your clothes inside out and this will confuse them long enough to allow you to make your escape. If a friend has been dragged into a fairy ring, toss one of your gloves inside and the revellers will disperse. To keep fairies out of your bedroom scatter flax on the floor, place your shoes with the toes pointing away from the bed and throw an old sock, the smellier the better, under the bed. A baptised child was safe against being carried off by the fairies, but before christening 'the little pagan' could be kept kept safe by having his father's trousers laid over the cradle.

Iron
Fairies are terrified of iron and they will vanish immediately on being shown any form of the metal. Keep a knife or a nail in your pocket and under your pillow at night. Hang open scissors over a baby's cot and the child will be quite safe from being kidnapped by fairies, if not from mutilation by falling scissors. A nail driven into a cow killed by falling over a precipice keeps the elves away. In Russia a scythe was hung over the house door at night. A horseshoe hung over the door will keep fairies out; it is usual to hang the horseshoe points up to keep the luck in, though in Dorset it is traditional to hang it the other way up.

In the children's game of tag, originally the one chasing was a witch or fairy. The players who were being chased could declare themselves "safe" if they could reach and touch iron.

Christian Symbols

Fairies are afraid of Christian symbols such as bibles and crucifixes; drawing a cross on cakes will stop fairies dancing on them. If a child is fairy-struck give it a cup of water in the name of Christ and make the sign of the cross over it. Churchyard mould scattered on the doorstep will keep fairies out. Fairies have no power on the Sabbath day of Sunday, and they even cannot bear to hear the name pronounced.

The bible was a relatively late form of protection against fairies, mainly because it was not until the nineteenth century that the bible became a common household item. But when this happened, it was almost instantly assumed that it held great power against the fairies. Interestingly, Gaelic translations of the Bible. used the term *leanan sith* (literally, "fairy lover", or more generally, "spirit consort") for one account of a supernatural creature (translated as "python" in English). The common people of Ireland and Scotland took this passage to be Biblical proof of the existence of fairies.

Pagan Symbols

There are a number of old Pagan symbols which will keep out fairies, such as a holed stone, or a pig's head or pentacle drawn on the door. A rowan cross tied with red thread will offer protection when hung in a high place in the house or byre. The besom or broom can be placed beside the hearth to prevent fairies coming down the chimney. A Witch Bottle [a glass bottle containing sharp objects such as nails and pins, ashes, salt and rowan wood] can be buried before the doorstep.

Bells

Church bells scare away fairies. After Halloween [October 31st] any crops left in the fields belong to the fairies, so bells used to be tolled all day on October 30th to make sure the little folk did not pre-empt their prerogative while the harvesters hurried to finish their work. The bells on Morris Men's costumes offer them protection from fairies and other spirits.

Oatmeal

If oatmeal is sprinkled on clothes or carried in the pocket no fairy will approach. In Mull mothers used to fill the pockets of boys travelling at night with it. If oatmeal is taken out of the house at night it is sprinkled with salt to prevent the fairies taking the substance out of the farmer's whole grain.

Mirrors

Fairies don't like to catch sight of themselves in mirrors, so a mirror facing any point where they might enter a house, such as opposite a door or window, will deter them.

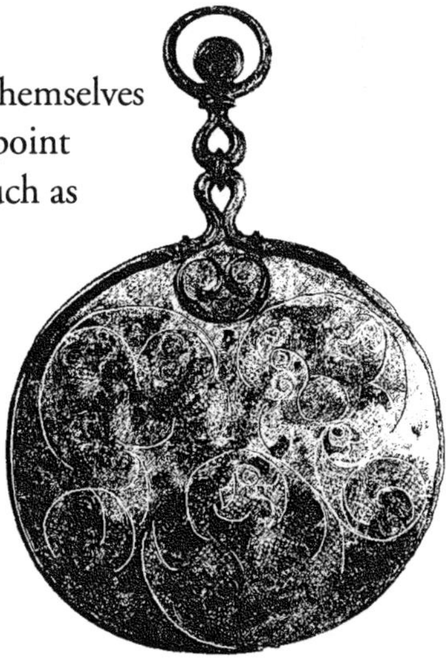

The Birdlip Mirror,
a fine example of
Bronze Age Craftsmanship

Baking

To prevent fairies taking the baking a final bannock is made with a hole through it, which is not toasted on the gridiron, but placed on a stone near the fire. A sieve should not be allowed out of the house after dark, and no meal produced unless sprinkled with salt.

Fairies like to steal querns or handmills. To prevent this they should always be turned deosil or sunwise [clockwise].

Plants

There are a wide variety of plants that protect against the attentions of fairies. Trailing pearlwort [known in Gaelic as *mothan* or *moan*] protects its possessor from fire and the attacks of fairy women. If fairies are stealing your milk, lace it with moan and it will render them powerless, as the Flora Scotica states:

'So long as I preserve the Moan
There lives not on earth
One who will take my cow's milk from me.'

St. John's wort [in Gaelic *achlasan challumchile*] wards off fevers and prevents the fairies carrying off people while they sleep. A twig of broom will keep fairies out of the house, while a gorse hedge will keep them off your property. In Scotland, heather is used to keep fairies and ghosts out of the house.

An Anglo Saxon remedy for fairy ills involves rubbing myrrh into wine with an equal amount of white incense [frankincense]. Shave a little off an agate and add it to the wine. Drink after fasting for three, nine or twelve mornings.

St. John's wort

When children are pining away and are fairy-struck, the juice of twelve leaves of foxglove were given [please note that this is poisonous]. Burning thorns on a fairy hill releases captive children,

On the last night of the year fairies are kept out by the holly decorations. The last handful of reaped corn should be made into a harvest maiden or corn dolly and hung up in the house to keep them out till the next harvest. Parents should adorn their children with bells or daisy chains to protect children on May Eve.

A mulberry tree in your garden will keep away fairies. At the dangerous times of Midsummer and Midwinter you should dance around it counter-clockwise- possibly the origin of the rhyme 'Here we go Round the Mulberry Bush'.

Ground ivy [*Glechoma hederacea*] is a magic charm against the unwanted attentions of fairies. One story tells of a young girl who was seized by fairies who tried to get her to join in their revels and drink their wine. She was saved by a red haired man who lead her out and gave her a branch of *Athair-Luzz* [Gaelic for ground-ivy] and told her to hold it in her hand till she got home, then no one could hurt her. She took it and ran home, though she heard pursuing footsteps. When she reached home she bolted the door and heard voices saying 'the power we had over you is gone through the magic of the herb- but when you dance again with us on the hill, you will stay with us forever more, and none shall hinder.' She kept the herb safe and the fairies troubled her no more, but for a long time she heard the fairy music.

Fire

Fire is the great preventative against fairy magic- a ring of fire will protect a child, a cow, a woman, a house or a man. The spirit of fire will destroy all fairy magic. Fire thrown into the water in which feet have been washed takes away its power to admit fairies to the house at night. Fire can be carried around laying-in women and round children before they are christened to protect them. If fairies are seen coming through the door burning embers should be thrown at them to scare them away. Pass a red-hot turf three times over and under the body of an animal that is fairy-struck, singeing the hair along its back, to drive off the fairies.

Urine

Stale urine can be sprinkled over cattle, doorposts and the walls of houses on the last evening of every quarter of the year to keep off the fairies.

Water

If you are being chased by evil fairies it is possible to leap to safety across running water, particularly a southward-flowing stream.

You can escape the Fairies on the islands of Scotland by descending to below the high-tide mark on the shoreline. The Fairies are unable to go below the high-water line.

CHAPTER SEVEN

Fairy Plants

The spots where fairies meet are rural and romantic in character. Shakespeare tells us that Titania's bower was:

A bank whereon the wild thyme blows
Where oxlips and the nodding violet grows,
Quite over-canopied with lush woodbine,
With sweet musk-roses, and with eglantine.

There are a wide range of trees and flowers that are particularly associated with fairies in one way or another. These include:

Elder *Sambucus nigra*

In Denmark, in former times, the elder was known to be under the protection of Hulda, the Elder Mother, and in England the Elder Mother or Elder Queen. She lived at its roots and was the mother of the elves. Whoever wished to take a branch or cut the tree had to first ask her permission, otherwise grave misfortune would follow. On clearing a field, elders were left standing and had to be ploughed around. Whoever felled an elder tree risked seeing his livestock carried off by sickness. In Lincolnshire it was thought that cutting elder wood without leave of the Old Lady or Old Girl offended her and permission must be sought:

'Owd Gal, give me some of thy wood and
Oi will give thee some of moine, when I graws inter a tree'.

According to popular lore, she did not like floorboards or furniture to be made of elder, and if a child were placed in an elder cradle it would not grow- Hulda would come and pull him out by the legs or the fairies would steal him.

According to Langland's *Piers Plowman* Judas hung himself on an elder tree and it is also said by some to have be the tree on which Christ was crucified. An old superstition stated that to burn elder logs was to bring the devil or evil fairies into the house:

Hawthorn bloom and elder flowers
Fill the house with evil powers

Elders were planted on new graves by the Welsh and Manx Celts. If it blossomed, the dead soul was thought to be happy in the Summerland.

It is safe to take a branch from the elder on January 6th without permission if you spit on the ground three times. This elder branch can be used to draw a magic circle in a lonely place for the purpose of demanding magic fern seed, which will give you the strength of thirty men. Hulda will see that an unseen hand delivers a chalice, containing the seed.

Foxglove *Digitalis purpurea*
The common name 'foxglove' may be a corruption of 'folksglove', the glove of the Good Folk or fairies who, like the flowers, inhabit the woody dells. This has given rise to many of the plant's folk names- Fairy's Glove, Fairy's Cap, Fairy's Thimbles, Fairy Petticoats, Fairy Weed, Little Folk's Gloves and Goblin's Thimbles. In Gaelic the foxglove is called the 'Thimble of the Old Fairy Woman' [*miaran nan cailleacha sith*] associating it with the hag fairy [see A-Z] or *Lusmore*. If you want to keep fairies away, you should remove any foxgloves from your garden.

Reed *Phragmites communis*
In Gaelic the reed is called 'the Distaff of the Fairy Woman' [*cuigeal nam ban sith*]. The Gaelic word '*gaothaiche*' also relates to the reed and means 'hollow'. It refers to the mouth of the bagpipe. The pipes were originally made from reeds and in Celtic legend the fairies invented the bagpipe. Because of its thick root the Celts identified the reed with a submerged dryad. Both the biblical Moses and the Celtic bard Taliesin were taken from the reeds after being set afloat shortly after birth.

In Greek myth the god Pan fell in love with a water nymph called Syrinx and pursued her until she reached the river Ladon, where she cried out to her sister nymphs to enable her to cross it.

Pan reached out to grasp her, but instead found his arms filled with reeds. Hearing the breeze as it passed through the reeds make a low musical sound, he plucked seven of them and made a pipe which he named Syrinx. The pipe had seven reeds in accordance with the harmony of heaven, which was said to contain seven sounds.

Fly Agaric *Amanita muscaria*

This red and white spotted mushroom is closely associated with fairies: perhaps that is why they wear red caps. The mushroom causes hallucinations and was used by witches and shamans to produce visions and to travel to the spirit worlds. The ancient Celts, among others, had a taboo on eating red food, which was believed to belong to the spirits or to the ghosts of the dead.

Fairy Ring Mushrooms *Marasmius oreades*
These rings of mushrooms, which appear on lawns and in meadows leaving a circular bare patch, are said to be a favourite dancing place of the fairies. It is now thought that some of these rings are as many as 600 years old. If someone sees a fairy ring and jumps into it they will die young

Hazel *Corylus avellana*
The hazel tree has many connections with fairies. A fifteenth century recipe for summoning fairies involved burying hazel wands under a fairy hill. The tree was called *bile ratha* in Ireland meaning tree of the rath [the abode of the sidhe]. Boiling jam was stirred with a hazel or rowan stick to prevent the fairies from stealing it

Hazel is the commonest wood used to make a forked divining rod. In Britain these were used for divining water and buried treasures, as well as guilty murderers. The divining rod was connected with elves and pixies who have all the treasures of the earth in their keeping. It was traditionally cut on St John's Eve, one of the great fairy festivals.

The fairies of English hazel thickets, who had names like Churnmilk Peg and Melch Dick, were said to inflict painful bloat and cramps on anyone who tore off unripe nuts, but they were probably angered more by the damage done to the trees than by the theft.

The sacredness of the hazel to the Celts is demonstrated by the death penalty that was carried out on anyone foolish enough to fell a hazel tree. An early Irish poem, the *Dindsenchas*, tells of Connla's well, which was located near Tipperary. Nine hazel trees overhung the well and they contained all the knowledge of the poetry, arts and science. The hazel nuts dropped into the well and were eaten by the salmon that swam there who developed one bright spot on his body for every nut he ate. Eating the nuts from these trees or the salmon itself confers knowledge and wisdom.

There is an ancient Celtic story which tells that Sinend, daughter of Lodan son of Lir, often visited a well in fairyland. There stood the hazels of wisdom and inspiration which in the same hour bore fruit, blossom and foliage which fell upon the well in the same shower. On one occasion the waters broke forth in anger and overwhelmed her, washing her up on the shore of the river Shannon where she died giving the river its name. This is a cautionary tale, a warning that the gifts of wisdom and inspiration may not be attained without a degree of risk.

Wild thyme *Thymus vulgaris*

At midnight on midsummer's night the King of the Fairies dances with his followers on thyme beds. In Shakespeare's A Midsummer Night's Dream Oberon tells Puck,

"I know a bank where the wild thyme blows
Where oxlips and the nodding violet grows."

It is an ingredient of many recipes dating from around 1600, which supposedly allowed one to see fairies. One charm states that to see fairies you should make a brew of wild thyme tops gathered near the side of a fairy hill and grass from a fairy throne.

Like other fairy flowers, wild thyme is unlucky to bring into the home.

Heather *Calluna vulgaris*

Fairies are said to feed on the stalks of heather. The plant is much associated with mountains, and bees love to drink from it. The honeybee, which orientates itself on its journey, from the heather to the hive, in relation to the position and angle to the sun, was regarded by the Celts as a messenger travelling the path of the

"I know a bank where the wild thyme blows
Where oxlips and the nodding violet grows."

sunlight to the spirit world.

An Irish myth tells of the death of the giantess Garbh Ogh [probably a hag goddess] who set up her chair in the womb of the hills at the season of the heather bloom and then expired.

White heather is a lucky charm and a protection against evil.

Ragwort *Senecio jacobaea*

Ragwort causes fatal poisoning in horses. Fairies sometimes bury their treasures beneath ragwort stalks and these weeds are used as mounts by fairies when they want to fly. The magic words to make them work are 'Horse and Hattock!' One Cornish man rode a ragwort to fairyland and back again.

Silverweed *Potentilla anserina*

This weed is turned up by the plough in spring. One of its old names was 'seventh bread'. It is said that fairies like to eat it and it is probably assigned to them because it grows underground.

Alder *Alnus glutinosa*

The alder tree grows near water and it is under the protection of the water fairies. The alder yields three dyes, red from the bark, green from the flowers and brown from the twigs, taken to represent fire, water and earth. The green dye is associated with fairies' clothes.

Bluebell *Hyacinthoides non-scriptus*

A bluebell wood is a place of fairy spells and enchantments. The presence of bluebells in oak copses is a sign that the malicious fairies the oakmen are present and mortals should be wary. Witches often grow bluebells to attract fairies, and at one time their presence in a garden was a damning piece of evidence in a witch trial.

Primrose *Primula vulgaris*
In Celtic lore the primrose is a fairy flower. It can make the invisible visible, and to eat primroses is a sure way to see fairies. If you touch a fairy rock with the right number of primroses in a posy [probably thirteen] it will open to fairyland and fairy gifts, but the wrong number opens the door to doom. A German legend tells how a little girl found a doorway covered in flowers, and touching it with a primrose opened it up, leading into an enchanted castle.

In Somerset, thirteen primroses were laid under baby's cradle to protect it from being taken by fairies. In Buckinghamshire on May Eve, primrose balls were hung over the house and cowshed door.

In ancient Celtic times, the primrose was regarded as a herb of immortality, associated with the spring goddess, holding within it the secret of eternal bliss. When its lore was Christianised the primrose was said to grant access to heaven.

Cowslips *Primula veris*
These lovely spring flowers are cherished and protected by the fairies. Cowslips are sometimes called Lady's Bunch of Keys or Culver's Keys, which unlock the doors to the fairy mounds of the West Country and the treasure beneath them

Four leafed clover *Trifolium sp*
I'll seek a four-leaved clover
In all the fairy dells,
And if I find the charmed leaf,
Oh, how I'll weave my spells!
The clover has always been highly regarded and associated with the Triple Goddess of classical myth, with the Celtic sunwheel and later with the Christian trinity. According to Christian lore the four leafed clover represents the cross and enabled the wearer to ward off evil and witches, to see fairies and spirits, to heal illness and gain good fortune. Four leafed clovers will dispel any fairy magic.

Hawthorn *Crataegus monogyna*
The hawthorn is a tree very much associated with fairies; their trysting places are under its shade. It is said that when the oak, ash and thorn grow close together it is a favourite haunt of the fey folk and those solitary hawthorns growing on hills or near wells are markers to the world of the fairies. Any human who sleeps beneath one, especially on May Eve, is in danger of being taken

away by them. In some parts of Brittany and Ireland it was considered dangerous to pluck a leaf from old and solitary trees especially those growing in unfrequented spots and on moorland. Fairies are very protective of hawthorns, and a blooming tree should never be trimmed as it angers them, and always the tree should be trimmed east to west.

Fern

Cornish pixies are said to be especially fond of ferns. One story recounts how when a young woman accidently sat on a fern a fairy man magically appeared. He then forced her to promise to watch over his fairy son, by having her kiss the fern and recite:

"For a year and a day I promise to stay."

For that period she was an inhabitant of fairyland.

Rowan *Sorbus aucuparia*

Rowan draws its name from the old Norse word *runa* meaning 'a charm'. The rowan is associated with protection, particularly from witchcraft, fairies and lightning. In the north of Britain sprigs were once fixed above cattle sheds to protect the animals and in a like manner over the doors of houses to protect the occupants from enchantment. Sprigs of rowan were also worn on the person to ward off the evil eye. As a protective charm rowan should be gathered at Beltane [May Day] and bound together with red thread to form an equal-armed cross. Boiling jam should be stirred with a rowan stick to prevent the fairies from stealing it.

Oak *Quercus robur*

The Romans believed that men, nymphs and fauns sprang from the oak. Fairies often like to dance around old oak trees. Wood-wives [German forest fairies] frequent the old sacred forests and oak groves. Some tribes once worshipped a wood-wife between Christmas and Twelfth Night. Her clothes were kept in an old oak tree.

Elves live in oak trees and the holes found in the trunks are their means of entrance and exit. A New Forest rhyme advises *'turn your cloaks for fairy folks are in old oaks'* [to turn your cloak inside out protects you from being distracted from your path by fairies].

In England unfriendly dwarfish creatures called oakmen live in the saplings which grow from felled oaks. If bluebells are present in the copse, this is a sure sign of their presence. Oakmen may offer food to passing mortals that will turn out to be poisonous fungi disguised by magic.

If an oak has to be cut down it should only be cut down during the waning moon and should be told about the forthcoming event. An acorn should be planted near to the old tree to provide a new home for the tree spirit.

Birch *Betula alba*

One of the main associations of the birch is with purification. Birch is also a protective tree, believed to guard a man or woman who carried a twig of it and to keep livestock safe when attached to their barn or shelter. In some parts of England a birch sapling was hung with red and white rags and leant against stable doors at Beltane (May Day) to prevent horses being 'hag-ridden', i.e. being taken out by fairies or witches and ridden.

The hallucinogenic mushroom the fly agaric grows beneath the birch. This may be why the birch constitutes the shaman's seven stepped pole. In Russia the forest spirits called Lieschi were considered to be always present in clumps of trees, particularly the tops of birch trees.

In Somerset, a female spirit called 'The One With the White Hand' flickers from birch copses, pale and gaunt as the trees, to ambush young men.

Blackthorn *Prunus spinosa*
In Ogham, the Druidic tree alphabet, the blackthorn was *straif* which translates as 'strife'. The words 'slay' and 'sloe' [the fruit of the blackthorn] are also closely linked.

A popular English fairy tale tells of a giant's daughter who fled with a prince, with the giant in pursuit. She felt her father's breath on her back and said to the prince: 'Put your hand quickly into the ear of the grey filly and throw behind you what you find there.' It was the point of a thorn and as he threw it a forest of blackthorns twenty miles long sprang up, so dense that scarcely a weasel could slip through and the giant had to give up the pursuit.

In the tale of Sleeping Beauty, a hedge of blackthorns sprang up around the castle but opened to allow the prince to pass. In another story, a wandering princess aided by a magic wand opened a path through an impenetrable blackthorn hedge. The evil man following her thought to pass through in his turn, but the hedge closed in on him.

In the tale of Rapunzel, the witch who had imprisoned her threw her suitor from the high tower. He fell onto a blackthorn and was blinded. He wandered for two years until Rapunzel, who had by that time escaped from the tower, found him. Finding him blind she wept, but when her tears fell onto his eyes he was instantly cured.

November 11th is recognised in Ireland as the day of the blackthorn sprites, the Lunantishees, otherworldly beings who guard the sacred blackthorn from any human foolhardy enough to profane the sacred tree by cutting the wood at this time.

Blackberry *Rubus fructicosus*
The bramble was a sacred plant of the Celts; in Scotland the bramble, along with the rowan and the yew, constituted the sacred fire.

A taboo on eating blackberries exists in Celtic countries. In Brittany and Cornwall the reason given is that the blackberry belongs to the fairy folk. In France some people still will not eat them as they are associated with the devil who enters into them after November 11th [Old Samhain].

Apple *Malus sp.*
The apple was one of the most sacred trees of the ancient Europeans; under Celtic law, to fell one was punishable by death.

In European mythology legendary fairy isles of apples are common, and always lie in the west, the place of the dying sun, from which it proceeds to enter the underworld, or Land of Youth, travelling through the realms of death in preparation for its rebirth at dawn. All Neolithic and Bronze Age paradises were orchards; 'paradise' means 'orchard'.

In British tradition the legendary Isle in the West was Avalon, which translates as the 'Isle of Apples', from the Welsh *afal* meaning 'apple'. King Arthur- who was originally a Celtic sun god- was taken there as he lay dying by Morgana ['Of the Sea'], the island spirit who guarded the apples of the Otherworld. To the Celts the afterlife was lived in a permanent summer, a land of the ever young, an apple orchard where the trees were always in fruit. The Greeks believed that the good spent their afterlife in Elysium, which means 'apple-land' or 'apple orchards'. It was a happy land of perpetual day and the inhabitants could choose to be reborn on earth wherever they elected.

Eating a fairy apple confers eternal youth, immortality or rebirth. However, gaining the fruit is fraught with danger. The tree is always guarded, usually by a snake or dragon. Once the fruit has been eaten, the hero can never return to being what he was before. The fairy queen warned Thomas the Rhymer about eating the apples in her garden. She said that to partake of the food of the dead is to know no return to the land of the living.

In the west of England the small apples left on the trees are called 'the pixies' harvest' and children used to be allowed to scrump them, even being encouraged with pennies or bread and cheese by the farmer's wife to do so.

Fungi

Toadstools, mushrooms and fungi, with their unearthly shapes and rapid growth, are often associated with fairies, as evidenced by some of their names, which include Yellow Fairy Club, Slender Elf Cap, Dune Pixie-Hood and Dryad's Saddle.

Red deer in particular are associated with fairies
and in Mull they are said to be their only cattle.

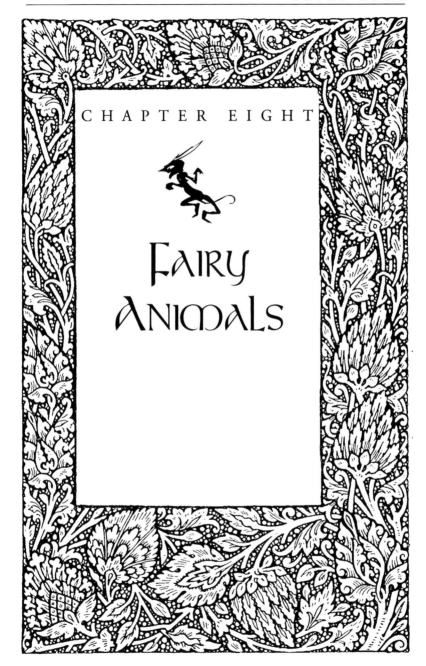

CHAPTER EIGHT

Fairy
Animals

Butterfly

In Celtic cultures the butterfly is an emblem
of the human soul, or perhaps a soul in
actuality. The ancient Celts wore butterfly
badges as a mark of respect for the ancestral
spirits. Celtic names for the butterfly include
Dealan-de, Tarmach-de, Dearbadan-de, each
containing the Scottish Gaelic for deity *'De'*.
Butterflies are also the symbol of the sidhe and fairies are often
pictured as riding on their backs. Mediaeval angels and fairies were
sometimes depicted with butterfly wings.

Cat

Fairy cats [*cait sith*] are of a wild breed, as large as dogs, black with
a white spot on their breast, arched backs and erect bristles. Some
say they are witches in disguise. The tailless Manx cats from the
fairy Isle of Man are said to have been bred by the fairies.

Perhaps the strange reputation of cats arises from their

association with many
ancient goddesses such as
the Egyptian cat headed
Bast or Bastet ['Soul of
Isis'] and the Roman
moon goddess Diana,
while Freya, the
Scandinavian goddess of
the moon, fertility and
love, had a chariot drawn
by cats. The Irish triple
goddess Brighid was
linked to a cat in an Irish
tale. In Scotland the Blue

Hag of Winter [*Cailleach Bheur*] was able to turn herself into a cat, like the shape shifting Welsh goddess Ceridwen.

The Celts believed that looking into a cat's eyes would enable you to see the fairies, or see into the Otherworld. In Mediaeval times the cat was considered the embodiment of evil fairies.

There is a Scottish legend of the Cait Sith, a fairy cat with dark green eyes and very long ears. Fairy cats keep appearing in Britain, sometimes the size of an ordinary cat, sometimes much larger and sometimes black. Kugarvad, King of the Cats, haunts Europe in the same way. The King of the Cats is often referred to in Celtic lore and was said to dwell as an ordinary cat by day living on the Isle of Man, and to travel the country at night as a royal cat to avenge any slights given to him during the day.

Cattle

Cattle played a vital part in the economy of earlier cultures, particularly the Celts. They were the source of food and wealth: the bride price and the price of slaves were set in cows. In Britain and Ireland cattle raids were a way of ensuring wealth and power. Because cattle were thought to be so important, they were the targets for envy. Witches and fairies were blamed for stealing milk from cows, either by making milking motions from a distance, or by taking the form of a hare or hedgehog to suckle from the cow. Elaborate precautions were taken to protect the herds. Rowan branches were passed over cows or tied in crosses with red thread and put in the byre. To protect cows in the stall the Irish and southern English scattered primroses on the ground.

Some fairies keep herds of cattle. Cows that have been found on the shore are called *cro sith* or 'fairy cows', because they are believed to be of no mortal breed but to live under the sea on seaweed. If one appears amongst an ordinary herd they grow frantic. The animal then enters a knoll, and if the vigilant farmer does not stop them, all the others will follow. Sometimes when fairies steal away a cow the appearance of the cow is left, but the substance is gone.

Otherworldly cattle are common in British lore, recognised by their red or round ears. A white fairy calf haunts the countryside around Liphook in Hampshire. A herd of cattle, said to be descended from fairy cattle, have grazed the parkland around

Chillingham Castle in Northumberland since the thirteenth century. They have the red ears and white coats of fairy cattle, and it is said that they will kill anyone who touches them. In Scotland fairy cattle would be left as gifts for mortals, identified by their round ears. In Ireland a sacred white heifer would appear on May Day to bring luck to the farmer. In other Irish tales white cattle are considered to be unlucky, as they are more likely to be stolen by fairies. Cracks in a cow's hide were said to be caused by 'elf bolts', shot at the animal prior to its abduction.

Fairy cattle were generous creatures that gave an unending supply of milk to their human owners. The freckled cow, Y Fuwch Frech, lived near Cerrigydrugian in Denbigh. She supplied the whole neighbourhood with milk, filling any vessel brought to her. Then one day a witch tried to milk her into a sieve, and continued to do so until the cow went mad and drowned herself in Llyn Dan Ychen.

Once a band of fairies haunted Llyn Barfog, a lake near Aberdovey. At dusk they appeared, clad all in green, accompanied by their milk white hounds. They also possessed milk white cattle called *Gwartheg y Llyn* or 'Kine of the Lake'. One day a farmer caught one of these cows and his fortune was made, it produced such butter, milk and cheese as was never seen. They called the cow Fuwch Gyfeiliorn and its fame spread. The farmer became rich beyond his dreams. One day he took it into his head that the fairy cow was getting old and he ought to fatten her for slaughter. They day came and despite the pleading eyes of the cow the butcher raised his arm and struck her a blow. Suddenly there was an almighty shriek and the bludgeon went right through the head of the cow and felled nine men standing close by. Then a green lady came from the lake and called the cow. It arose and went to her and disappeared back beneath the waters, never to be seen again.

An ancient belief was that if a man gave a gift of a cow to the poor, at his death the spirit of the animal would return to guide him to the Otherworld.

Boar

The boar was once considered to be a very magical creature, associated with spirits, gods and fairies. It was also a symbol of the fertility spirits of the earth. In Germany when the corn waved it was said 'the boar is rushing through the corn'. The last sheaf of the harvest was often called the 'sow' and was saved and baked into a loaf in the shape of a boar at midwinter, which was placed on the festive table until the end of the Yuletide season. It was then put away and kept until the spring sowing when part was eaten, and part mixed with the corn.

The magical boar is instrumental is the death of vegetation and corn gods, who are killed and often dismembered only to be resurrected later on: in Egyptian myth the god Set [as a boar] killed the vegetation god Osiris, lover of the goddess Isis; in Greek myth Apollo [as a boar] killed the vegetation god Adonis/Tammuz, lover of the goddess Aphrodite; in Irish myth Finn Mac Cool [as a boar] killed Diarmuid, lover of Grainne; an unknown god as a boar killed King Ancaeus, devotee of the goddess Artemis in his vineyard; Attis was slain by a boar, while the ancient Cretans said that Zeu was ripped apart by a boar and buried in their midst.

The Celts venerated the boar as a sacred animal connected with prophecy, magical powers and with the protection of warriors. In Celtic myth the swineherd holds an honoured position, and most of them are also magicians. In the story of the 'War of the Bulls' Marvan , which means 'Black Raven [which may be another name for Morvran/ Afagddu the son of Ceridwen], is the royal swineherd to King Guaire of Connaught. He has a magical white boar which is his physician, bard and messenger. The jealous bards of the palace persuade King Guaire to kill it. In revenge Marvan takes on the bards in a contest of wit and withers them into silence.

Boars and swine were amongst the most powerful animals of the Celts and stories of them include Henwen 'the white ancient sow', guarded by Coll mab Collfrewy; the swine of Pendaran Dyfed, guarded by Pryderi, son of the Lord of the Underworld; the two magic pigs of Lubhdan; the pig of Tuis which was healing and wine producing; Mukka Slangha ['the health giving pig'] which had nine tusks in each jaw, and which, when killed, provided many warriors with magic food, while red swine were encountered on an Otherworld island by Mael Duin.

In northern Europe a ghostly boar was said to lead the wild hunt through stormy midwinter skies [ordinary boars dislike wind and are said to be able to predict it].

Cuckoo

The cuckoo is *eun sith* or 'fairy bird', the bird of Tir-nan-og, coming from the words of the god Angus Og and flying first to the Isle of Lewis, along with the other birds. She will never build a nest in case the gods will not let her return. The cuckoo is said to go to the mysterious realm of the Land of the Dead in winter, entering the fairy mounds.

The arrival of the cuckoo marks the arrival of spring. In Sussex it was said that spring started when 'the Old Woman' [probably a hag goddess of winter] shook the cuckoos from her apron.

Cuckoos bring good luck or bad luck, depending on what you are doing when you first hear them; whatever you are doing you are fated to do for the rest of the year. If you are in bed you will become ill and bedridden. If the call comes from the right, it is good luck for the year, make a wish and it will be granted, but if the call comes from the left it is a bad omen. If you are looking at the ground you will be dead within the year.

Deer

The stag was one of the four sacred animals of the Celts and has played an important part in folklore in many areas of the world. Antlers have been found buried at Newgrange and sites in Glastonbury and at Stonehenge.

Red deer in particular are associated with fairies and in Mull they are said to be their only cattle. Tradition says that no deer is ever found dead with age and the shed horns are never found because the fairies hide them. Fairy women often assume the form of red deer. Fairies dislike deer hunters and throw elf-bolts at them. When a slain deer is carried home at night the fairies press down on the bearer's back until he feels as though he is carrying a house. Should he stick an iron or steel knife in the carcass it will become light again.

During the winter, the stag herds are said to be protected by the Cailleach or Hag and her women, who herd and milk them.

Remnants of an ancient British stag cult may be seen in the legend of Herne the Hunter, possibly a British stag god equivalent to the Gaulish Cernunnos. Herne the Hunter is said to still haunt Windsor Great Park and to ride out with the Wild Hunt at the midwinter solstice. He is described as a mighty, bearded figure with a huge pair of stag's horns on his head. He wears chains, carries a hunting horn and rides out on a black horse accompanied by a pack of ferocious hunting hounds.

Dog

Fairy dogs [cu sith] act as guides to the fairy realms and lead people into the underworld. They are usually green or white with red ears or in Wales white dogs are considered to be fairy dogs. In Eastern Europe fairy dogs are said to have white rings around their necks and to carry fairies around at night. The fairy dog makes its lair in the clefts of rocks and travels in a straight line. It barks only three times, and by the time the third bark is heard the victim is overtaken, unless he has reached a place of safety.

Fin Mac Coul's dog Bran was of the fairy breed and was described as having yellow feet, black sides, a white belly, a green back and red ears. Bran's venomous bite killed whatever it struck. When at speed he appeared as three dogs and once simultaneously intercepted three deer at three passes.

Several legends of Britain tell of the Wild Hunt, a pack of ghostly dogs who fly through the night sky to pursue their quarry. The hunt was known to the Saxons as *Einherier* or *Herlathing* and is also called the Wisht Hounds or Dartmoor Hounds. The leadership of the hunt has been ascribed to Herne the Hunter, King Arthur, the Devil, Charlemagne, Gwyn ap Nudd, Odin and Woden. The prey is variously a white stag, a white boar, white-breasted maidens or the souls of the damned. Some say the hounds are the souls of unbaptised children.

Even ordinary dogs are thought to be able to see ghosts, spirits and fairies. They hate fairies and chase them, but when they return all the hair is scraped off their bodies and they die soon after.

Snail

In Ireland the snail was called 'the pookah's spit', probably because its horns were similar to those of Puck or a pookha. Its slimy white trail of course resembled spit, and the pookah was said to spit or defaecate on wild fruit at Samhain, rendering it unfit to eat. Any such whitish liquid found on the ground was associated with the underworld people as in some accounts fairies had white blood. In Victorian illustrations fairies are frequently depicted riding on the backs of snails.

Frog

For the Greeks and Romans the frog was an attribute of Aphrodite/ Venus as fertility and lust, but also harmony between lovers. In the fairy story a girl kisses a frog which transforms into a prince, a symbol of sexual awakening.

The Celts called the frog 'the Lord of the Earth' and associated it with healing waters and used frogs in cures for many ills. There is an ancient healing spring at Acton Barnett, in Shropshire, where the fairy guardians of the well appear as frogs. The largest of the three is addressed as the 'Dark God'.

Pig

The pig, with its large litters, is a fertility symbol, hence lucky charm pigs and piggy banks.

The *Mabinogion* states that the first pigs were a gift to Pryderi from the King of the underworld. The sea god Manannan kept a magical herd of pigs in his underworld kingdom, each animal killed and eaten at night would be reborn in the morning. Any human eating them would be made immortal. However, the water the pigs were cooked in would not boil until a truth was spoken for each quarter of the pig. Pigs were thought to be otherworldly creatures and their flesh formed the feasts of the underworld and were therefore taboo food in the ordinary world. Swineherds were held in great esteem by Celtic society.

There are tales of fairy pigs in the Isle of Man and at Andover in Hampshire a spectral pig is seen on New Year's Eve.

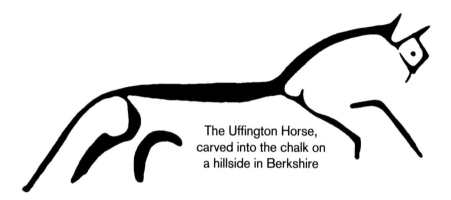

The Uffington Horse, carved into the chalk on a hillside in Berkshire

Horse

Fairies are very interested in horses. When horses neigh at night they are being ridden hard by fairies or witches.

The horses of the Tuatha de Danaan were stabled in the hollow hills. They were made of fire and flame and were as swift as the wind. They were shod with silver and had golden bridles. A cavalcade of Sidhe knights had seven score steeds, each with a star-like jewel on its forehead, and seven score horsemen, all king's sons, clad in green mantles fringed with gold, wearing golden helmets and carrying gold spears. The horses lived for one hundred years. The last of them was owned by a lord of Connaught, but was sold at his death. Refusing to be mounted by its base born buyer, it threw him to the ground and bolted, never to be seen again.

There are many stories of water horses called *each sith*, 'the unearthly horse' or 'fairy horse'.

Bat

Because of its nocturnal habits the bat is associated with night , witches, fairies and the powers of darkness. The Mediaval church saw bats as symbolic of the devil, and Satan was often depicted with the wings of a bat. In 'The Tempest' Shakespeare describes Ariel as flying on the back of a bat, and fairies are sometimes shown with bats' wings.

Goat

For the ancient Greeks and Romans the goat represented virility: goats are fertile and reputedly lusty. The Greek god of the wild, Pan, was the son of Amalthea ['goat']. Both he and and his satyrs had the legs, horns and beards of goats. Russian wood spirits are said to appear as part human but have the ears, horns and legs of goats. In Ireland 'goat-heads' were evil spirits associated with leprechauns and the Formorians. Goats were sacred to various Celtic deities and to fairies like Bucca and Puck.

Fairies are said to comb goats' beards every Friday, or perhaps Wednesday. English country people said that it was not possible to see a goat for twenty-four hours continually, as at some point he must go and visit either the fairies or his master the devil to pay homage and have his beard combed.

Christianity equated the goat with the devil, the damned and sinners. It was the symbol of agility and obstinacy and from it we get our word 'caprice', from the Latin for goat, Capricorn.

Eagle

The power and strength of the eagle associate it with authority and royalty. Scottish chieftains wore three eagle feathers in their bonnets, as do fairy princes in legend.

The grave of Arthur in Snowdonia is said be guarded by a pair of eagles carrying chains. The Druids were thought to have adopted the forms of eagles and a gathering of three score eagles [druids] took place on an island at Loch Lomond each year at Beltane to augur the omens for the coming year.

The Celts saw eagles as emblems of old knowledge. In the search for the young god Mabon the eagle was second oldest animal on earth and pointed the way to the oldest, the salmon, who knew where Mabon was.

Woodpecker

At one time
it was thought
that the woodpecker
could be used to obtain the
mysterious herb springwort, which could open doors
and locks. If the woodpecker's hole was blocked up the
bird would fetch some of the herb to unblock it. If a
piece of red cloth were placed below the nest, the bird
would think it was fire and drop the sprig onto it. The woodpecker
could also be watched to see where it fetched the plant from. In
tales it can tell where fairy treasure is hidden, it knows where
medical herbs are to be found, guards them and threatens to peck
out the eyes of anyone who steals them.

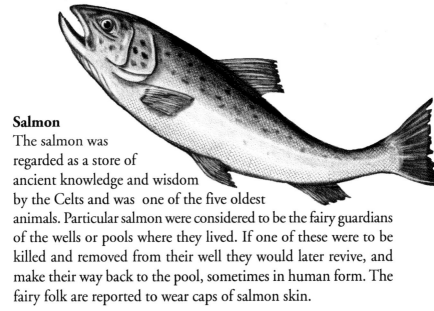

Salmon

The salmon was
regarded as a store of
ancient knowledge and wisdom
by the Celts and was one of the five oldest
animals. Particular salmon were considered to be the fairy guardians
of the wells or pools where they lived. If one of these were to be
killed and removed from their well they would later revive, and
make their way back to the pool, sometimes in human form. The
fairy folk are reported to wear caps of salmon skin.

Hare

The hare was sacred
to the ancient Britons
and has long been a
familiar of fairies
and witches.
The fearsome
fairy hag,
Black Annis
is associated
with a hare.

CHAPTER NINE

Changelings

Come away, O human child!
To the waters and the wild
With a faery, hand in hand,
For the world's more full of weeping than you can understand.
W.B.Yeats,'The Stolen Child'

Fairies often steal human children and leave changelings in their place. Some say that they do this because the fairy families need to interbreed with humans to strengthen their bloodlines. Others say that it is because every seven years the land of the fairy has to pay a tithe to hell, and human captives are used as payment. The changeling [*sithbheire* in Gaelic or *Plentyn-newid* in Welsh] left in the place of the human child is an ugly fairy baby or just a piece of wood that seems to be alive for a moment. Should the replica not die it will soon reveal its fairy origins.

The Sure Signs of a Changeling

A changeling may have a wizened or deformed appearance. It will probably be thin, weak or ailing and will cry continually. It may have a voracious appetite, be fond of dancing, be unnaturally precocious or make some unguarded remark as to its age. In Ireland left-handed children are said to be changelings

Of course, these signs often meant that in the past any sick child was suspected of being a changeling and poor human babies were subjected to the terrible methods of detecting a *sithbheire*.

Making a Changeling Reveal its Nature

There are several methods of making a changeling reveal its true nature. These include placing the suspect baby on a shovel and holding it over the fire saying-

' *Burn, burn, burn- if of the devil burn;*
but if of God and the saints be safe from harm'.

Alternatively you could expose the baby to the weather on a dunghill all day. The changeling is converted into a stock of wood by saying a powerful rhyme over it, or sticking it with a knife. It can be driven away by running after it with a red hot ploughshare, by getting between it and the bed and threatening it with a sword, by leaving it out on the hillside and paying no attention to its screams, by sprinkling it with urine, or by dropping it in the river.

To detect a changeling it may be best to send for a fairy doctor who will prepare a drink of certain herbs [a childless woman is best to make the potion]. Should there be no improvement the wise woman will instruct the mother to place the child for three nights running on a shovel outside the door from sunset to sunrise. During this time it will be given foxglove to chew and cold water will be flung over it to banish the fire devil. The screams of the child will be frightful, but the fairy doctor will assure the mother to have no fear, the fairies are tormenting the changeling but by the third night their power will cease, and the child will be restored.

[However, the unfortunate baby will undoubtedly be dead by then.]

The method of finding out a changeling by means of eggshells is very widespread. Empty eggshells are arranged round the hearth and as the curious changeling gets up to examine them he will peer into each saying-

'This is but a windbag; I am so many hundred years old
and I have never seen the like of this'.

An alternative method is to go through the motions of brewing water in halves of eggshells. The changeling will sit up and declare-

'I have seen the egg before the hen,
I have seen the acorn before the oak,
but I have never seen brewing in an eggshell before!'

thus revealing its ancient age. It should be thrown onto the fire and laughing and shrieking it will fly up the chimney. The true baby should then be found at the door.

There were several other rather sadistic methods of gaining back a child. Some were beaten with with iron implements, or taken away and left exposed on the windward side of a fairy hill or tumulus. There were a number of recorded instances in 19th century Ireland where parents treated their children in such a manner when they suddenly took ill, or turned out to be "simple" or were born with deformities.

A couple of the parish of Trefeglwys in Wales lived in a cottage called *Twt y Cwmrws* ['The Place of Strife']. They could not agree whether or not their twin babies were changelings. Eventually, they called in a cunning man to resolve the matter and he advised them to boil an egg shell and offer the egg shell stew to the harvesters in the nearby fields. As soon as the egg shells were boiling, the two babies exclaimed:

'Acorns before oak I saw,
An egg before a hen,
But never one hen's egg stew

Enough for harvest men.'
The mother then knew the twins to be changelings and threw them into a lake. A troop of fairies instantly appeared to rescue the fairy children, and returned the stolen human babes to their parents.

Returned Children
Sometimes, even when the changeling has not been detected, the fairies will return stolen children, especially if they grow up ugly. However, it usually needs human interference, as in the following story.

A man on his way to work saw two women going up to a house and heard one say to the other

'There is a beautiful boy unguarded in this house, go in and hand it out to me and we will leave this dead child in its place'.

The man surreptitiously watched the two women carry out

their evil scheme and realised that they were fairies at work. As the fairy-women stood gloating over the bonny human baby he leapt up and made the sign of the cross over the sleeping infant. The two fairies immediately screamed and fled.

The man took up the child and tenderly carried it away to his wife. He told her to look after it and to be careful to keep a turf fire beside the cradle to keep the fairies off.

Hurriedly returning to the scene of the kidnap he heard a keening coming from within the house. Going in, he asked the weeping woman what was wrong. Wiping away her tears she replied that her poor child had died in the night.

'Be comforted,' returned the man 'the dead child is a changeling, and your own child is safe.' He instructed her to lay the dead body on the fire, which she did, saying

'Burn, burn, burn, if of the devil, burn, but if of God and the saints, be safe from harm'. As soon as the changeling felt the fire it sprang up the chimney and disappeared.

Some fairies even seem to have motherly instincts of their own. Once when a mother bent over a withered changeling the latch lifted and in came a fairy with her real child.

'It was the others who took it' she said. All she wanted was her own child back.

Parents were not always successful in getting back their child. In fact it was ironically considered lucky to have a fairy child in the house, for the fairies, always mindful of keeping a bargain, would often do the family good turns to compensate for the theft. The cattle would always be full of milk and the churn would never sour. Changelings rarely grew to maturity. In many cases, they were believed to not live past the age of seven, in others they might survive into puberty, but not into adulthood.

How to Stop Fairies Kidnapping a Child

Fairies readily seize unbaptised children, therefore lock all the doors, windows and presses and if the fairies are already inside let them stay there until the proper precautions are taken. A red-hot coal should be placed under the cradle and a rowan branch or implement of iron or steel should be placed above it. The child should be wrapped in its father's shirt. A protective charm can be made by tying up a white feather and some hair from a black cat in a red ribbon, and hanging it round the neck of the child.

For I am gone to the fairy people.
Make the most of that other child
Who prays with you by the village steeple
I am gone away to the woods and wild.

I am gone away to the open spaces,
And whither riding no man may tell;
But I shall look upon all your faces
No more in Heaven or Earth or Hell.

Lord Dunsany, 'The Fairy Child'

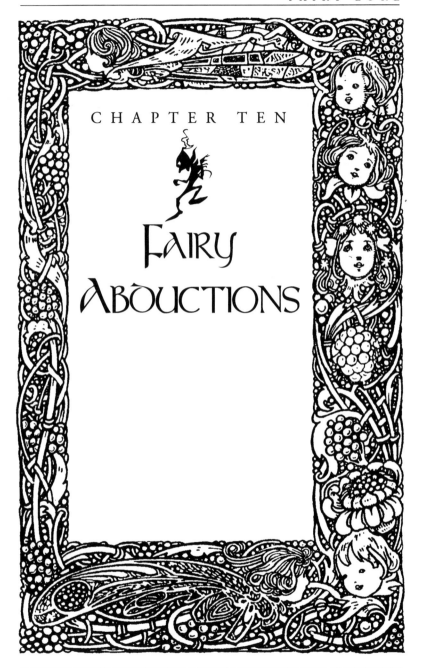

CHAPTER TEN

Fairy
Abductions

Fairies also abduct adults, and in this case they usually leave behind a stock, a wooden image that is animated for a few days by magic. When the spell wears off the likeness grows rigid and relatives assume that the person has died. Sometimes the fairies content themselves with taking away the spirit and leaving the body behind.

Women not yet risen from childbed are especially vulnerable. To prevent kidnapping by fairies, women should not be left alone during their confinement. It is traditional for the female relatives and neighbours to gather in the house and watch for eight days. A row of nails may be driven into the front of the bed, a smoothing iron or reaping hook placed under the bed and in the window. An old shoe is put in the fire. The doorposts should be sprinkled with urine, the bible opened and the breath blown across the woman in bed. Mystic words and threads are woven about the bed, and when the midwife leaves she places an oatmeal cake with a shoe on it in front of the bed. If the wife's spirit is taken away she will become silent and vacant. In this case her marriage gown should be thrown over her. If the fairies appear at any time, water in which an ember was extinguished or burning peats should be thrown at them to drive them away.

Human midwives are sometimes spirited away to deliver a fairy baby. The serving maid Eilian of Garth Dorwen ran off with the Tylwyth Teg [the Welsh 'Fair Folk']. Nine months later her old mistress, the midwife of Llandwrog, was summoned to a birth. She was taken to a large cave in which there was a magnificent room, with a woman on a fine bed. After the birth the husband asked the midwife to anoint the baby's eyes. As she did so her own eye began to itch and she rubbed it, accidentally getting some of the magic ointment into it. Instantly she saw that the cave was really small and poor and that the wife was on a bundle of rushes and withered ferns. She recognised Eilian, her old servant. Some weeks later she encountered the fairy husband in the market place at Caernarfon, and asked how Eilian was getting on. He enquired which of her eyes had she seen Eilian with? When she told him he put it out with a bulrush.

At Loch Ranza on the Isle of Arran, a midwife was harvesting oats, when she noticed that a neighbour was about to kill a big, yellow frog. Feeling pity for the creature, she saved its life. The next day, a beautiful boy on a grey horse road up to her house, and informed her that the frog had been the Queen of the Fairies in disguise. She was summoned to the Fairy Mound, where she delivered the Queen of a child.

When the fairies leave home in companies they travel on eddies of wind, known in Gaelic as *oiteag sluaigh* or 'people's puff of wind'. People on night journeys have been lifted by these winds and spent the night madly careering through the skies. On being dropped to earth they return to the house they last left, too stupefied to recognise the house or its inhabitants. Others find themselves on some distant hill, or in some inaccessible place they could never have reached on their own. Even in daylight some have been carried from one island to another, in great terror lest they fall into the sea. By throwing one's left shoe at the *oiteag sluaigh* or a knife, or soil from a mole hill, or one's bonnet, the fairies are made to stop what they are doing and return whatever they are taking away.

Fairy men often abduct women for wives and lovers. Handsome girls must be guarded or the fairies will carry them off for brides.

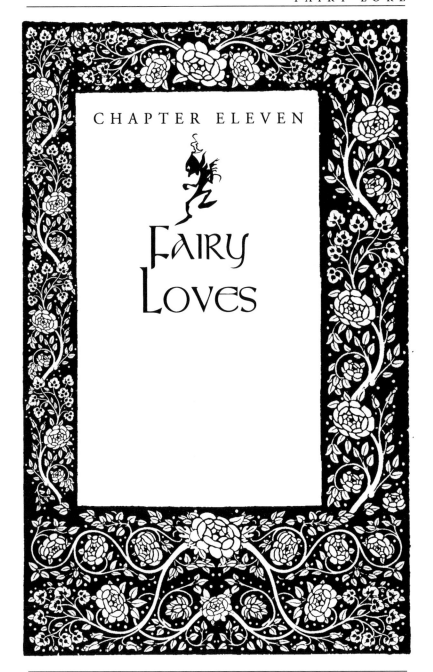

CHAPTER ELEVEN

Fairy Loves

There are many tales of humans who have married or become the lovers of fairies. It is said that fairies are jealous of the human race who have souls, and are often tempted by mortal men and women or perhaps they want to strengthen their white blood with the red blood of humans. These relationships always have conditions and taboos imposed on them, such as the fairy should never be struck or touched with iron, or seen on a certain day. Should the fairy lover leave for any reason, usually because of the breaking of a taboo, then the human spouse will pine away and die.

The fairies can assume any form they like and often appear at village festivities as tall, dark, noble looking men to charm young girls as dancing partners. Afterwards the girl will move with a special fairy grace and then fade and die, and everyone knows that her soul has been carried away to Tir nan Og where she will become the bride of a fairy king. If a man is tempted to kiss a *Sigh-oge*, or young female fairy, in the dance he is lost forever, and can never leave fairyland.

Some marriages with fairies work out well, though if either of the couple should touch the other with iron they will both become old and die. In the Orkneys Magnus O'Kierfea took a fairy bride in addition to his own mortal wife. On festival nights such as Halloween, Christmas and New Year's Eve he would be sure to set a place for her and the food would always be gone in the morning. With her aid he became a famous healer and they had three daughters.

A fairy chief went to Kirwan of Castle Hackett, the great Connaught chief, and asked his help against a hostile fairy tribe that had invaded his territories. This was granted and men and fairies plunged into the lake and defeated the enemy. The Connaught men were rewarded with presents of gold and silver while Kirwan received a fairy bride. All of his female descendants were noted for their unearthly beauty.

The children of such unions have a mystic nature, possess second sight and generally become famous in music and song, but they are passionate and vengeful. Their beautiful eyes and bold reckless temperament betrays their fairy blood. Many famous people are thought to have had one mortal and one otherworldly parent. These include Alexander the Great, the Queen of Sheba and Merlin. Even Shakespeare was said to have been part fairy.

The Test of Love

One of Arthur's knights, Launfal, fell in love with a fairy maid. She agreed to appear whenever he wished on condition that he must never speak of her or summon her when others were present. Her name was Tryamour, meaning 'test of love'.

Queen Guinevere noticed the handsome young knight and tried to seduce him. He refused and she exclaimed that he was not fit for a woman's love. He replied that he was beloved of a lady whose lowliest handmaiden put the queen's beauty to shame. In one unguarded retort, he had therefore both broken his promise to the fairy maid and insulted the queen.

She complained to Arthur that Launfal had tried to violate her and the young man was immediately arrested. Though he put his case and most of the knights sided with him it was decreed that he must produce his mistress within one year or die. Of course, the fairy would no longer come, and one year later he stood waiting in the courtyard to be executed on the pyre. Then through the gate, riding on a white horse, the fairy Tryamour appeared. All agreed that he had spoken truthfully and the two lovers rode away together to fairyland. The lady was never seen again, but Launfal appears once a year to look on the world of mortals that is now denied to him.

The Lay D'Ywenec

The Breton *Lay D'Ywenec* tells of a rich old man who was governor of Caewent. Desirous of an heir he married a young maiden. Because of her beauty he grew excessively jealous and determined to keep her safe from other men. He shut her up in a tower to which no one had access, except himself and his sister.

She was immured there for seven years. During this time she bore no children and passed her time lamenting her lonely fate. One April the lord set out on a journey, leaving his wife to curse her parents and bemoan the fact that though her husband was old he seemed hale and hearty and showed no sign of dying soon. She wished she could have been a lady wooed by a gentle knight, as in the minstrels' tales.

Just then a goshawk flew into the room. Settling, it turned into just such a handsome and gentle knight. At first she was afraid, but he spoke to her courteously and said he had been in love with her for a long time, but could not come to her, unless she wished it. His told her that his name was Eudamarac and that she only had to wish for him, and he would appear, but to beware of the old woman who watched her closely, for if they were discovered it would mean his death.

The lady soon began to radiate such an aura of happiness that her husband marvelled at the change and began to suspect that his sister had betrayed his trust. However, she reassured him and they began to plot how to watch the girl and discover her secret. The old man told his wife that the king had sent for him, and that he would be away for a while. As he set off his sister hid behind a curtain to see what would happen.

The girl immediately wished for her lover and the old woman witnessed all that passed. When the lord returned she related all she had seen and he caused metal pikes to be placed at his wife's window. The next day he set off hunting and the eager bird flew to the girl, but failed to notice the sharp spikes and was cruellyimpaled on them, mortally wounded. Still, he struggled bleeding into the chamber and threw himself on the bed. He comforted the girl, saying that she would bear him a son who would be handsome, brave and wise, and that he should be her solace. Having said this he flew off.

The lady jumped out of the window after him and pursued his trail of blood, eventually coming to an entrance in a hill. She went in and found herself in a fair meadow. In the distance was a city made of silver, surrounded by marshes, forest and waters upon which three hundred ships sailed. She followed the bloody spoor through the town to the castle, finding no man or woman. At the castle she entered a low chamber and found a knight sleeping there, but knew him not. She passed on to a larger chamber, where another knight lay sleeping. She passed on to a third chamber where her lover lay in a gold bed.

Seeing him she swooned, but he consoled her, telling her that she should leave, lest his people took their revenge on her for his death. He gave her a ring, which he said would make her husband forget all that had happened. Then he gave her a sword, which was to be given to their son when he became a knight, which would cause him to know of his birth and heritage. He gave her a fine dress of silk and induced her to leave, but she had not gone far when she heard the death knell tolling.

He husband remembered nothing of what had passed, and in due time she gave birth to a son, named Ywenec, who grew up beautiful, generous and valiant. After he had been dubbed a knight the family was summoned to a feast at Caerlyon. They stopped at an abbey and were shown a stately tomb, covered with a rich embroidered tapestry with twenty tapers burning, and censers made of amethyst. They learned that it was the tomb of a king who had died at Caerwent for the love of a lady, leaving the throne vacant.

The lady heard this and cried to her son that it was the tomb of his father, wrongfully slain by the old man. She then gave him the sword and told him the whole story, and in doing so expired on the tomb. Filled with rage the youth struck off the head of the old man and thus avenged both his father and mother. The lady was laid in the tomb with her lover and Ywenec was acclaimed king.

Aine

According to legend, Aine the fairy was sitting one day by Lough Gur [Ireland] when the Earl of Desmond chanced to see her and instantly fell in love with her. She agreed to marry him on the condition that he was never surprised by anything that their children did. Unfortunately when their son, the Earl of Fitzgerald, jumped in and out of a bottle he couldn't help his amazement and poor Fitzgerald turned into a wild

goose and flew away, while Aine fled into the mound still known as Knock Aine.

Melusina

Elinas, King of Albania married the fairy Pressina with the taboo that he should not witness her laying-in. She bore him the triplets Melusina, Melior, and Palatina. The king, forgetting the taboo, rushed in to see them, and the fairy and her daughters disappeared.

They went to the mysterious Lost Island, where the girls grew up. When they were fifteen, Melusina determined to be revenged on her father and set out for Albania with her two sisters. By magic, they imprisoned him and all his wealth inside a high mountain. Pressina was outraged and cursed Melusina to become a snake every Saturday until she should marry a man who would agree never to see her on that day. Melusina wandered the world and eventually arrived in the forest of Colombiers in Poitou, where all the fairies welcomed her and made her their queen.

It chanced that Count Raymond was travelling in the forest and arrived at the Fountain of Thirst, also called The Fountain of the Fays. There he saw three comely fairy women disporting themselves, the loveliest of which was Melusina. Naturally they fell in love and were married, with the condition that Raymond should not see her on a Saturday. Their marriage was happy, despite the fact that their children were all horribly deformed. However, it was not to last. The Count wondered why he could not see his wife on a Saturday and began to suspect that she had a lover. Concealing himself in her chamber he saw the horrible truth. Before his eyes she transformed into a writhing serpent, grey, white and blue. Still, the he loved Melusina and knew that if he ever revealed that he was aware of her secret she would have to leave him.

It then came about that one of their sons, the base Geoffrey, burned his brother and a hundred monks to death as they sheltered in an abbey. As Melusina went to comfort her husband he cried out 'Go, thou foul snake, contaminator of my race!'. Thus, the entire evil destiny that had lain in abeyance came to pass. Melusina told her husband that she must leave him and spend her time in pain and misery until Doomsday. She added that when one of her race was about to die at Lusignan she would appear, and when the castle was about to gain a new lord she would appear hovering in the air, or in the Fountain of Thirst.

Penelop

Near to the village of Beddgelert in Wales is a place that the locals call the 'Land of the Fairies'. It was once commonplace to hear the lovely music of the fairies there, and see their dancing and mirthful sports. A youth lived in the vicinity. He was brave and determined, and spent many evenings watching the fairies. One evening he spied them on the shore of Llyn y Dywarchen and his eyes were drawn to one of the fairy ladies. Her skin was like alabaster, her voice as lovely as the nightingale's and as unruffled as a zephyr in a flower garden on a summer's noon, her feet moved as lightly in the dance as the rays of the sun on the lake. He instantly fell passionately in love with her. So powerful was the youth's desire that he ran headlong into the throng. He seized the fairy maiden in his arms and bore her into his house. He bolted the door with iron so that the pursuing fairies could not enter.

Now the youth began to plead his cause to the exquisite lady. With soft words he wooed her. At first she would not hear of it, but in due time, seeing that he would not allow her to return to her people, she seemed to relent. She said that she would not marry him, but would become his servant if he could guess her name. He agreed, but guessing all the names he could think of got him no nearer his goal. All were wrong.

Then one night he was returning from the market at Carnarvon when he saw a number of fairies ahead of him, near the path. He thought that they might be planning to rescue their sister and decided to creep up close to them and endeavour to overhear what they were saying. As he did, he found that they were indeed speaking of the abducted fairy. One of they cried out pitifully 'Oh Penelop, Penelop! Why didst thou run away with a mortal?'

The youth returned home and called out 'Penelop, come hear.' The fairy lady came to him in astonishment and asked who had betrayed her name. He said nothing and she began to weep and bewail her fate. However, she was true to her word and began work in earnest, cleaning, washing, spinning, weaving and keeping the farm better than any housewife in the district. The holding began to prosper and the young man pestered her to marry him. Finally she agreed with the condition that if he should ever touch her with iron, she would return to the Fair Folk.

So they were married and for several years lived quite happily together. She bore him two children who were as lovely as fairies themselves. Then one day the couple went out to catch a filly in the field. Together they drove the it into the corner and the youth attempted to throw the bridle over it. But alas, his wife chanced to move into the way and the iron bit caught her cheek. She vanished immediately and was never seen again.

The Fairy of Llyn y Fan Fach

One day, a young man was grazing his cattle on the banks of Llyn y Fan Fach, when he saw a lovely fairy maiden sitting on the shore, combing her hair. He thought that he had never seen a woman as beautiful, and tried to entice her to come to him by offering her gifts of bread. She smiled and shook her head, but this only made him more determined.

Eventually, after many attempts, he persuaded the fairy to marry him. She warned him that if he should strike her more than twice, she would vanish forever. As her dowry, her father bestowed upon the couple many fairy sheep, goats and cattle, which all emerged from the lake at the call of the fairy woman.

The couple were married, and for many years lived happily on a small farm near Myddfai and had three lovely sons. One day, the couple were preparing to go to a Christening, and the man asked his fairy wife to fetch the pony, while he fetched something from the house On returning, he found her still standing in the same spot. Fearing they would be late, he tapped his wife on the shoulder and told her to hurry up. She turned and looked at him with a sad expression, for he had struck her once.

A few months later they went to a wedding, and the fairy burst into tears. Embarrassed, the man struck her on the shoulder and bade her be quiet. She turned to him and said 'I am weeping because their troubles are just beginning, and so are ours, for you have struck the second blow.'

This frightened the farmer, and he took care not to strike his wife again in the years that passed, until one day they attended a funeral and his wife burst out laughing. Engaged, he tapped her on the shoulder and asked what was the matter with her. She replied that 'When people die, their troubles are over, and so is our marriage, for you have struck the third blow.' With that she disappeared into the lake, taking all her fairy animals with her. The farmer never saw her again, but she returned occasionally to instruct her sons in the art of herbs and medicine. They became the famous physicians of Myddfai.

CHAPTER TWELVE

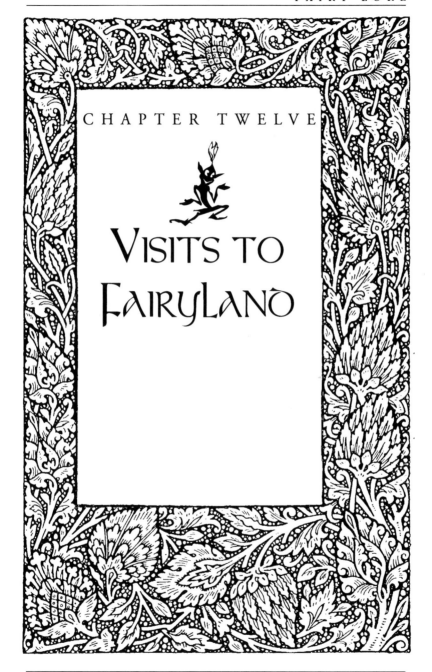

VISITS TO FAIRYLAND

There is a Welsh tale of a man who spent time with the fairies. One morning he heard a bird singing sweetly and sat down to listen to it. When he rose, after what he thought was a few minutes, he was surprised to find the nearby tree withered and dead.

He hurried home but his house had changed and an old man whom he didn't recognise was there. The young man asked him what he was doing there, and the old man exclaimed how dare he insult him in his own house.

'In your house!' cried the young man. 'Where are my father and mother, who I left a few minutes ago, while I listened to the most charming music under yonder tree, which when I arose was withered and leafless, and all things too seemed changed?'

The old man asked him his name, and the young one replied 'John'. Then the old man realised who he was, and said that he had often heard John's father, who was his own grandfather, speak of him and bewail his absence. 'But old Catti Madlen of Brechfa had said that you were under the power of the fairies and would not be released until the sap of the sycamore was dried up. Embrace your nephew, dear uncle!' The old man attempted to embrace him, but as he did so John shrivelled and crumbled into dust.

Tam Lin

This famous ballad concerns a maiden called Janet who went into Carterhaugh Wood in the Scottish Border country. She wished to pick wild roses near a certain well that lay in a clearing there. No sooner had she plucked a single blossom than a tall, handsome elf appeared before her. The pair dallied together all that afternoon and fell in love. The elf told her that he was really not a fairy at all, but a human knight under enchantment, held in bondage to the Fairy Queen. His name was Tam Lin, and he was the grandson of the Earl of Roxburgh. Janet determined to rescue him, an endeavour that her lover explained was possible, but full of danger. The following Samhain Eve Janet proceeded to the crossroads and hid behind a thorn bush, to await the passing of the Fairy Rade. Eventually, to the sweet sound of the music of lutes and pipes, a procession came into view, led by the lovely Queen riding a black horse, and followed by pale fairy lords and ladies. Among them was Tam Lin on a white horse, recognisable by the fact that he was wearing only one glove. As instructed, Janet sprang out from her hiding place and pulled him from his saddle.

By malignant fairy glamour Tam Lin was transformed into a salamander lizard, and Janet nearly lost her grip. Then the lizard became a huge, coiling snake. Janet was terrified, but hung on. The serpent became a bear, but she held it fast. The bear became a swan, which flapped against her breast. At last, its struggling stopped and Janet found that she held only an iron bar. This was the end, she knew, and cast the bar into the well. There it steamed and a moment later a naked man stepped from the well, her lover Tam Lin become human again.

The Fairy Queen blazed with anger. She turned her gaze on

Tam lin, amazed that a mortal woman could have bested her. She cried that had she known that he could have been won by a mortal woman, she would have torn his heart from him and given him one of stone. At this she wheeled away, all her band following, and disappeared into the trees

Thomas the Rhymer

Another mortal who spent time in fairyland was Thomas the Rhymer. He had been playing his lute in the woods when a beautiful fairy riding a horse had emerged from the trees to listen. Eventually she dismounted and he tried to kiss her. She warned him that such an act would bind him to her for seven years, but he did not hesitate. They journeyed together through the night to a bright meadow in which there were two paths, one to perdition and one to righteousness, but the fairy queen explained that for lovers and singers there was another path, a twisting third way that led to fairyland.

After seven years Thomas returned home but his songs were sweeter and more poignant than ever before. He was also able to foretell the future, as in fairyland he had eaten an apple whose flesh had the power of truth, a parting gift from the fairy queen.

On his seventy-eighth birthday he was holding his annual party when he was told that two white deer, a male and a female, were heading through the village to his house. He knew this to be a summons to fairyland and followed them back there, where he still sings and plays.

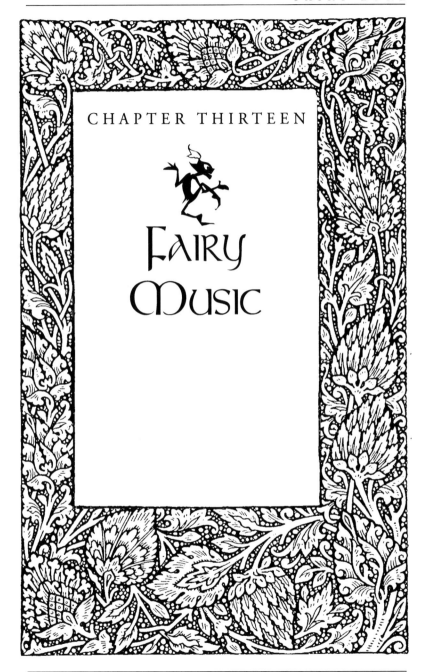

CHAPTER THIRTEEN

Fairy Music

Fairies charm people down to their realms with fairy music or *Céol-Sidhe*, and no one who has heard it can resist its power and are fated to belong to the fairies forever. If you put your ear to a fairy mound, you may be able to hear the unearthly strains of lovely music. There is such a mound on the Isle of Skye called *Sithean Beinne Bhoidhich* ['Fairy Home on the Bonnie Hill']. Music also comes from a burial cairn near Glen Elg in Scotland where the MacCrimmons, a famous family of pipers, are reputed to be buried.

It is dangerous for a young girl to sing when she is alone by a lake, for the spirits will draw her down to sing in the fairy palaces and she will be seen no more. Yet sometimes, when the moonlight is on the water and the waves break against the crystal columns of the fairy palace, you can hear her voice and know she is singing to the fairies.

Sometimes mortals do not get drawn down into the earth, but the spell remains on them, and they are haunted by the music until they die. They always have a spirit look for the fairy music is low and plaintive, a fatal charm for mortal ears. One man slept on a rath and was haunted by the music till he had no peace and threw himself off a cliff into a lake. A gentleman entered a cabin in County Clare and there a young girl was singing a melancholy song, without words or structure. She told him that she had heard the fairy harp and those who hear it lose their memory of love and hate, and never more have any sound in their ears save the soft music, and when the spell is broken they die.

Many young girls have been drawn away by the music and have danced all night with the fairies, though they are found fast asleep in bed in the morning. They remember all they have seen, and while they were with the fairies they learned the secrets of love potions, spells and charms.

There was a girl who saw things no one else did and heard music no other could, for the fairies carried her away at night and she danced with King Finvarra. One day she told her friends and asked them to go with her; she would put a salve on their eyes so that they could see the wonders.

When they got to the rath she instructed them to 'put your foot on my foot and look over my left shoulder and you will see the king and queen and all the others dancing on the grass, but take care not to make the sign of the cross, or speak the name of God, or they will vanish away, and perhaps your life will be in danger'.

On hearing this her friends ran away in fear, but the girl stayed and the next day told her friends that she had danced all night and heard the sweetest music. She wished she might live forever with the fairies on the hill. The girl died soon after and on the night of her death sweet music was heard floating around her house.

Beautiful flowers grew on her grave, though no hand had placed them there, and shadowy forms would gather to sing a low chant about it.

In the Western Isles one evening in late November, the month when spirits have power over all things, a pretty girl went to the well for water and slipped and fell. When she got up everything round her had changed. She saw a crowd round a blazing fire, staring at her and she was afraid.

A beautiful youth approached her and asked her to dance. She replied there was no music. At this he made a sign with his hand and exquisite music surrounded them as they danced all night. Eventually the music ceased and he invited her to supper. Instantly, a flight of steps appeared which spiralled down into the ground.

The gay company processed down to a large hall, bright with gold and silver lights, where a sumptuous banquet was laid. Everyone pressed her to take some wine, and she took the golden cup held out. Just then a red haired man whispered to her

'Eat no food and drink no wine or you will never reach your home again.' So she laid down the cup and refused to drink. The assemblage became angry and tried to force her to drink. She was saved by the red haired man who lead her out and gave her a branch of *athair-luzz* [ground-ivy]. He advised her to keep it in her hand until she got home and no one could hurt her.

She took it and ran, though she heard pursuing footsteps. When she reached home she bolted the door and heard voices saying 'The power we had over you is gone through the magic of the herb- but when you dance again with us on the hill, you will stay with us forever more, and none shall hinder.'

She kept the herb safe and the fairies troubled her no more, but for a long time she heard the fairy music.

Tudor of Llangollen came across fairies dancing to a fairy fiddler. He tried to resist the music, but eventually joined in saying 'Now play away, old devil!' and a pair of horns appeared on the fiddler, and a tail, and the dancers turned into cats, dogs, goats and foxes and they danced until the next day, when his master found him dancing madly alone. Pious words broke the spell and Tudor went home.

Many famous musicians learned their art by sleeping on raths, and the fairies would often gather round to listen to them, invisible to the human eye. Carolan, the celebrated bard, acquired his skills by sleeping out on a fairy hill at night when the fairy music came to him in his dreams and he played the air from memory. He then had the power to make men laugh or cry.

Numerous old Irish tunes are fairy songs such as 'The Pretty Girl Milking the Cow' and 'The Londonderry Air'. It is unwise to sing or whistle such tunes near a rath as the fairies don't like to hear their music on ordinary mortal lips.

Little Sister, whom the Fay
        Hides away within his doon,
Deep below yon seeding fern,
        Oh, list and learn my magic tune.

Long ago, when snared like thee
        By the shee, my harp and I
O'er them wove the slumber spell,
        Warbling well its lullaby.

Till with dreamy smiles they sank,
        Rank on rank, before the strain;
And I rose from out the rath,
        And found my path to earth again.

Little Sister, to my woe
        Hid below among the Shee,
List and learn the magic tune,
        That it full soon may succour thee.
Alfred Perceval Graves, 'Mor of Cloyne'

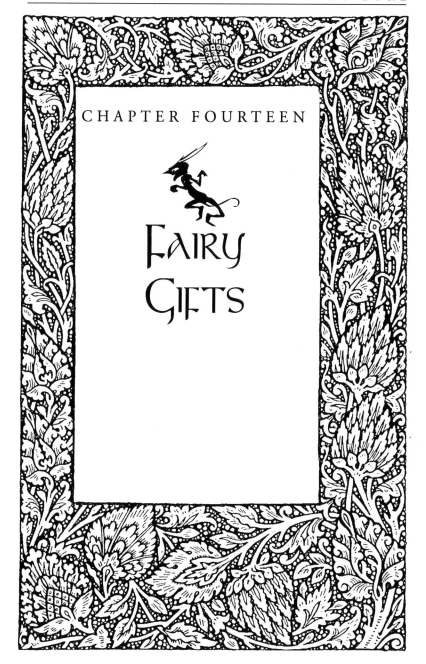

CHAPTER FOURTEEN

Fairy Gifts

Fairies can bestow almost any gift or skill on their favourites, such as skill in music, magic, prophecy or healing. Fairies are known to be capable of working very hard, spinning, weaving, baking, churning and building or working as gold and silver smiths or metal workers. If a smith, wight or other craftsman catches fairies working with his tools he can compel them to bestow on him the *ceaird chomuinn* or association craft, that is, assistance whenever he needs it.

Should a mortal borrow fairy utensils or food he will cause offence if he tries to return more than he borrowed, while fairies always return favours with a bonus. Fairies always return two measures of barleymeal for one of oatmeal, and if this is kept in a place by itself it proves an inexhaustible supply, providing the bottom of the vessel is never made to appear, no questions asked, and no blessing pronounced over it. At the thirteenth century church at Frensham in Surrey there is a huge cauldron which local people say was borrowed from the fairies but never returned. For this reason the fairies would never lend the village anything again.

In 1684 Captain George Burton, in his book *Pandaemonium*, reported the case of the Fairy Boy of Leith. The boy had amazing powers of second sight, which he said were given to him by the fairies. Every Thursday he visited them at Calton Hill, near Edinburgh. The entrance to the hill was only visible to those with fairy gifts, and once inside, the boy joined in the revels, playing a drum for the fairies to dance to. Sometimes they all flew off to France or Holland for the evening. Captain Burton and some friends tried to keep the boy in conversation one Thursday evening, but despite all their efforts, the boy slipped away to keep his appointment with the People of the Hills.

There is a flag called the *Bratach Sith* or 'Fairy Banner' which belongs to the MacLeods of Skye. The faded brown silk flag is still kept in the drawing room of Dunvegan Castle. There are several legends as to how the flag came into the possession of the clan. Some say that a McLeod married a fairy and she gave her husband the flag on the Fairy Bridge when she had to return to her own kin. Others say that a crusading MacLeod received it as a gift from a water sprite in the Holy Land, or won it from a she-devil. Yet again, the MacLeods trace their ancestry back to King Harald Hardrada, a Norseman who set out to conquer England in 1066 with a magic talisman called Land-Ravager, a flag which guaranteed victory to its possessor. However, it does not seem to have worked for Harald, who was defeated by the English King Harold. Land-Ravager disappeared after the battle, but may have come into the possession of the MacLeods.

Legend says that when the fairy banner is unfurled in battle, victory always attends it, but it can only be used three times. The clan have used it twice, on both occasions against their enemies the MacDonalds, once at Glendale in 1490, and again at Waternish in 1520. Whenever the flag was taken into battle, whether it was unfurled or not, twelve champion swordsmen were chosen to defend it. During the Second World War, many young clansmen carried a photograph of the flag with them.

There are several conditions surrounding the use of the flag. At least a year and a day must elapse before each summoning of fairy help, and if a pregnant woman should see it she will be taken in premature labour, while cows will cast their calves.

During the fifteenth century, the wife of the chieftain Iain Borb gave birth to a child. A fairy came to the castle, wrapped him in the flag and sung him a lullaby. When she left, the nurse remembered the words and melody, and since then, no nurse had been appointed to the MacLeod heir unless she knows the fairy song.

Fairies posses a great deal of treasure and sometimes share it with humans who do them a good turn, or those they take a fancy to. A young Danish girl once saw one of the Bergfolk mounds teeming with green beetles, and when she took two home they turned into gold coins.

Fairies often send for human midwives to help with the births of their children. They reward these women with gold. The Russian Dyeduska Vodyanoy lures girls into his underwater realms in order to marry them, and when they are about to give birth he will fetch a human midwife who will be rewarded for her services with gold or silver. These Finnish Kirkonwaki ['Church Folk'] fairies live beneath the altars in churches. When the females are experiencing a difficult labour, should a Christian woman lay her hand on the altar all will be well, and the fairies will reward the woman with gold. A German midwife was taken to a hidden chamber and attended the birth of an elf. The fairies kept her with them for a few days, but eventually she was allowed home, and given as her reward the sweepings behind the door. She arrived home and her husband was overjoyed to see her again. Then she emptied her apron onto the table and the sweepings had turned into a big pile of gold.

Fairy gold cannot be stolen but has to be given freely or it will turn into withered leaves, coal or bits of rubbish. The Korreds (male Breton fairies) always carry purses full of gold, but if a human steals it this turns into leather and hair.

To get the leprechaun's legendary pot of gold away from him, you must see him before he sees you. There is a tale of an Irish boy from Castlerea who loved books and wanted to find a pot of gold to buy more. One evening he found a leprechaun under a dock leaf and grabbed him with a view to appropriating his treasure. The leprechaun said there was no need for violence, they were cousins once removed; the boy was a changeling and only those with fairy blood could possess the gold.

The leprechaun took the boy to the old fort of Lipenshaw and led him through a secret door in the stone wall. The floor of the room inside was covered in gold pieces. The leprechaun told the boy 'Take what you want, but when the last glow of the sun vanishes, the gold will vanish also'. The lad loaded his pockets with as much gold as he could and was just going back for more when the door shut. He banked the money in Dublin and became rich and learned.

Another leprechaun showed one farmer the single ragwort in a field under which there was gold. The man marked it with a red ribbon while he went to get a shovel. When he came back there was a red ribbon on every ragwort.

However, fairies use their gold to tempt greedy humans. The Dracae (Scottish water fairies) float gold cups or jewellery on the surface of the water to try to tempt people to reach for them. Should a human do so they will be seized and dragged into an underworld realm where they will be enslaved.

Fairy gifts should not be questioned or they will be lost. Two farmworkers of Child's Ercall in Shropshire saw a strange creature rising from a pond. They prepared to flee but when the creature spoke they realised it was a mermaid. She told them there was a treasure in the pond and they could have as much of it as they liked, if only they would come into the pond and take it. They waded into the pond and the mermaid surfaced with a lump of gold as big as a man's head. One of the astonished labourers exclaimed that he had never had such luck in his life, but the mermaid was offended by his remark and she and the gold disappeared, never to be seen again.

Fairies take a great interest in human affairs. They like luxury and have contempt for those who penny pinch, especially those who drain the last drop of milk from the churn or strip all the fruit from the trees leaving none for the fairies. They punish kitchen maids who do not sweep the hearth clean and put out clean water for bathing fairy babies with pinches, cramps and lameness, while conscientious maids are rewarded with money in their shoes and good luck.

One Irish story illustrates how fairies sometimes interfere with human behaviour. There was a man in Shark Island who crossed to Boffin to buy tobacco, but when the weather was too bad his temper frayed and he used to beat his wife. One day a man came to him and said

'What will you give me if I go to Boffin and bring you tobacco?'

'Nothing' replied the man, 'whichever way you can go so can I'.

'Then come with me to the shore,' said the mysterious man 'and I'll show you the way across, but only one can go, so you must go alone'. As they approached the strand they saw a company of horsemen and ladies and heard the convivial sounds of music and laughter.

'Spring up on a horse and you will get across' cried the mysterious man. The other did as he was told and in an instant the company jumped to Boffin. He nipped off to buy his tobacco and returned to the retinue as quickly as he could.

Again he sprang onto his horse, but this time when everyone jumped they unaccountably stopped midway between the two islands, landing on a great rock. Whatever they did the horses could not be persuaded to go on. The company held a council and realised that there was a mortal among them. They rapidly came to the conclusion that they must drown him.

They roughly seized him and threw him off the rock. When he

surfaced and tried to scrabble back onto the rock they grabbed him and were about to throw him down again when a red haired man intervened. Picking him up, he carried the dripping mortal safe to the shore.

'Now you are safe, but mind the spirits are watching you. If you ever again beat your wife you will die on the rock as sure as fate'.

From that time the man was meek and kind to his wife and they both lived happily to a great old age.

Round about, round about,
In a fair ring-a,
Thus we dance, thus we dance,
And thus we sing-a,
Trip and go, to and fro
Over this green-a,
All about, in and out,
For our brave Queen-a.
The Elves' Dance', Anon

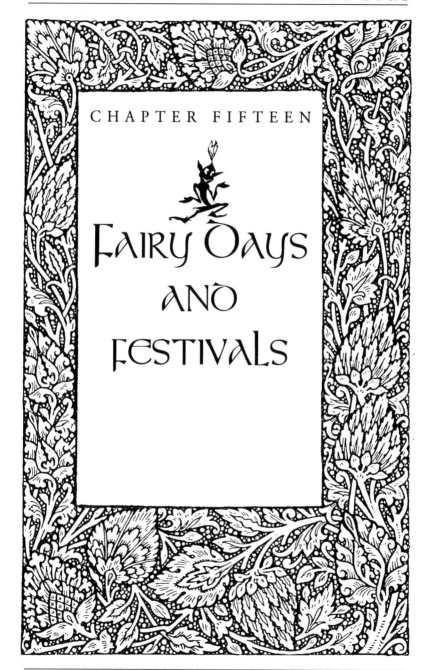

CHAPTER FIFTEEN

Fairy Days and Festivals

Friday

On Fridays fairies have the most power: it is their Sabbath day. Knives should not be sharpened on a Friday, as this will make the fairies angry. According to the Gaels, Friday should not even be called by its proper name [*Di-haoine*] but referred to obliquely.

Friday is an unlucky day to start a new job, begin a journey, or hold a wedding, for the fairies are out to cause mischief and will spoil it if they can. It is on this day that they are most often up to their tricks with elf-bolts, milk stealing and changeling swapping. On Fridays they are also wont to kidnap young girls as brides. After seven years the girls grow old and ugly and are sent back to the human world but with the compensation of a knowledge of herbs, philtres and secret spells to give them power over men to kill or cure. In this way the witches and fairy doctors achieve knowledge.

A fairy story told on a Friday should be prefaced by the words 'A blessing attend their departing and travelling! This day is Friday and they will not hear us'. This prevents Friday ill will coming on the narrator.

Wednesday

Some say that the fairies' special day is Wednesday, rather than Friday.

The Vernal Equinox

At the spring equinox, as the weather starts to brighten and the earth blossoms, a number of fairies start to become more active. The Domoviyr [Russian cellar spirits] shed their skins and grow lighter ones for the summer and should not be approached at this difficult time. The Russian river spirits, the Rusalkys, appear bathing in lakes and sitting on the shore combing their hair in the moonlight.

In Scandinavia fairies are most active at the festival of Ostara, the spring equinox. If they are denied their rightful portion of the festival feast you will have to give them twice as much at midsummer or you will be troubled until the next Ostara.

Beltane

Good fairies are most active from Beltane [May Day] to Samhain [Halloween]. The Cailleach Bheur [the Winter Hag of Scotland] gives up her struggle and allows summer to chase away winter. In Leicestershire, the Black Annis [the Winter Hag fairy of Leicestershire] hunt used to be held every May Day to chase the summer hare.

All fairies hold great festivals at Beltane and try to steal the ritual fire and fresh butter made by humans for the celebrations. In Arthurian legend Guinevere, thought by many to be of fairy origin, rode out a maying, dressed in fairy green.

The Lunatishee [the Irish Blackthorn Fairies] guard the sacred thorn and will not allow it to be cut on May 11th [old Beltane].

Every seventh year on May Eve fairies fight for the rights to the harvest, for the best ears of grain belong to them.

Midsummer

On Midsummer Eve, when the bonfires are lighted on the hills, the fairies are at their most frolicsome. It is one of the great Trow festivals. Fairies try to pass around the Baal fires in a whirlwind to extinguish them, but may be kept off by throwing fire at them. Humans can protect themselves from fairies by leaping through the fire and their cattle by driving them through the embers, passing glowing coals three times over and three times under the body of each animal.

The Irish spirit the Amadan-na-Briona is most active during the time of the summer solstice, playing mischievous tricks on people and precautions should be taken against the crop eating German fairies the Pilwiz.

Lughnasa

Lughnasa or Lammas marks the start of the harvest and the German Kornbocke causes grain to ripen, while the Russian Polevik kicks awake harvesters.

Fairies often hold processions or move house at Lughnasa and sometimes a line of lights can be seen moving from one hill to another.

The Autumn Equinox

The Autumn Equinox marks the time of Harvest Home, and the fairies have to be honoured and given their share. In England the Apple Tree Man has to have the last of the crop left on the ground for him and the Hazel Nut Fairies punish those who steal from their trees.

Samhain [Halloween]

Samhain marks the start of winter, and the ancient Celts celebrated it as a festival of the dead. After this, good fairies such as the Tuatha de Danaan and the English Puck retire from sight until Spring returns. Evil fairies, such as the Scottish Unseelie Court, become very active from now till Easter. Goblins are most seen at Halloween when they consort with ghosts. The Jimaninos of Mexico dance amongst people at The Festival of the Dead. Evil omens such as black fairy dogs and the Bean-nighe or Washer at the Ford appear.

Fairy mounds open at Halloween and you might get a glimpse inside. At Hollantide [11th November- old Samhain] the Hillmen or Hogmen, the most feared of the Manx fairies, move their abode, and one should not venture out then. They use well-trodden paths running in straight lines between the mounds

After Halloween, all the crops left unharvested belong to the fairies. In Ireland, Halloween is called Phooka Night and after this time he renders all the crops unfit to eat and spoils all the blackberries. Welsh gryphons blight any crops left in the field after Halloween and the Lunatishee will not allow blackthorn to be cut on November 11th [old Samhain]

Hag fairies make their appearance after Halloween. These were once probably crone goddesses of winter who ruled over the season. In Russia Father Frost starts spreading ice and snow.

The Winter Solstice [Yule]

At Yule, particularly in Scandinavian and Germanic countries, a wide variety of present giving fairies appear. The Italian Befana, the Icelandic Jola Sveinar, the Danish Julenisse, the Swedish Jultomte and of course Father Christmas deliver gifts.

The Icelandic Jubuk visits houses at Christmas and between Christmas day and Twelfth Night the German Frau Holda rides about in a wagon. Berchte ['bright one'] appears between Christmas and the New Year looking after spinning and destroying any left unfinished.

The Greek Callicantzaroi fairies gather to celebrate the solstice, staring at the sun and vanishing on Twelfth Night.

In the Orkneys the Trows leave the underworld and dance and in England the Wild Hunt rides out.

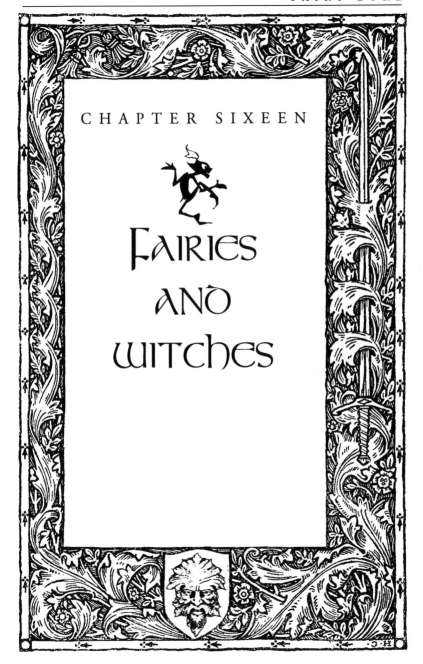

CHAPTER SIXEEN

fairies and witches

In legend and lore witches and fairies have many things in common. Both use elf-bolts, both steal milk from cattle, both have magical powers and both use herbs to poison, curse or cure. In many instances, witches were said to gain their powers from fairies. The young girls that fairies carry off for brides grow old and ugly after seven years and are sent back to the human world, but with the knowledge of herbs and philtres and secret spells to give them power over men.

James Walsh, a Dorset witch convicted in Exeter in 1566, admitted he learned how to bewitch people from fairies. He said he visited them in their mounds and spoke with them between the hours of noon and one, or at midnight. In 1613 Isobel Halfdane of Perth was carried from her bed into the fairy hills where she spent three days, learning the secrets of witchcraft. John Stewart was initiated into the magical arts on the hills above Lanark, and an Orkney witch confessed that she saw fairies rise from Greinfall Hill on their way to a feast at Yule. The famous Scottish witch Isobel Gowdie

"went into the Downie hills: the hill opened and we came to a fair and large braw room in the day time There are elf bulls routing and skoyling there at the entry, which feared me"

Anne Jeffries lived at the time of the English Civil War. One day she was knitting in an arbour when six tiny, handsome men appeared, the finest one had a red feather in his cap. They began

to kiss and caress her and when one touched her eyes she was transported to fairyland, where she seemed to be the same size as the other inhabitants. She was courted by all six men, but stole away with her favourite red-feathered beau. The others followed with an angry cloud and the world turned black and she found herself back in the arbour. She became famous as a clairvoyant and healer until she was arrested as a witch in 1646. She was not fed while in prison but the fairies sustained her. Eventually she was released, but spoke no more about fairyland.

Witches are the only people who can communicate with fairies with impunity. They are on good terms with each other and witches are frequent visitors to the fairy hills; being accused of such visits was enough to secure a conviction as a witch during the persecutions. Witches also grow many of the fairy plants- such as foxgloves and bluebells- in their gardens or gather them from the wild to attract their fairy friends, or to use them in their spells. At one time, even the presence of such plants in a garden was enough to warrant an accusation of witchcraft.

In Germany elves were said to be the children of witches and the devil. They could appear as caterpillars and butterflies and as they bored into a tree or ate the leaves, so the hearts of people the witches desired to injure were troubled.

PART TWO

What are Fairies?

T ales of small spirits and fairy-like creatures occur all over the world in every culture. They are non human creatures dwelling on the fringes of the spirit realms, whose existence sometimes impinges on and affects the human experience. They generally live underground in caves or burial mounds and possess magical powers. It is dangerous to eat their food.

Compare the South African Abatwa, tiny fairies that live peacefully with the ants in anthills but who are very shy, only occasionally revealing themselves to wizards, young children and pregnant women and the Cornish Muryans [From the Cornish *murrian* meaning 'ant']. These are tiny fairies. Some believe that fairies end their days as ants since every shapeshifting operation reduces them in size. In Cornwall it is thought to be very unlucky to kill ants, as they might be the final forms of tiny fairies.

The fairies are often euphemistically referred to as 'The Good People' in Britain and Ireland. The Yumboes, West African Senegal fairies are entitled *Bakhna Rakhna* or 'The Good People'. They live beneath the hills where they feast and enjoy dancing. The yumboes are hospitable and have invited many humans to their revels. They are seated at richly furnished tables and served by attendants who are completely invisible, except for their hands and feet. Yumboes go out at night to the nearby villages and steal the corn that women leave unattended. They are two feet tall with pearly skin and silver hair.

In Ireland the *Daoine Sidhe* ['People of the Hills'] dwell beneath the hills and burial mounds. They are fond of feasting, dancing and music. Several humans have visited their realms and the fairies emerge at night to attend village revels or cause mischief. Any food left out at night is said to belong to them.

A belief in fairies has persisted down the ages to the present day. In the eighteenth and nineteenth centuries folklorists and writers such as the brothers Grimm, W.B.Yeats, John Gregory Campbell, Thomas Keightley and Lady Wilde set out to systematically collect and record fairy lore. In the early twentieth century wide popular interest was sparked when two young cousins, Frances Griffiths and Elsie Wright, claimed to have photographed fairies in their garden. Though the figures looked remarkably like painted illustrations many people at the time were convinced that they were genuine, including Sir Arthur Conan Doyle, the author of Sherlock Holmes and noted spiritualist. Later both girls admitted that the photographs were fakes. In the 1970s the Findhorn Foundation in Scotland claimed that the remarkable growth of their vegetables was due to the kind offices of plant devas or nature fairies, and the place became a centre of pilgrimage for many.

There have been various ideas as to the origins of fairy myths and these have varied according to current fashions in religion, folklore interpretation and anthropology. What follows is an exploration of several of these theories.

King James I's book Daemonologie equated fairies with devils
and advised people who had them in their homes to get rid of them.

CHAPTER SEVENTEEN

Fallen Angels

According to Christian doctrine any spirit entity that is neither saint nor angel is demonic in origin. King James I's book *Daemonologie* equated fairies with devils in no uncertain terms and advised people who had them in their homes to get rid of them immediately. Writing in 1701 the Orkney vicar Rev. John Brand said that fairies were evil spirits seen dancing and feasting in wild places.

According to this school of thought fairies are fallen angels, cast out of heaven for their pride. Some fell to earth and lived there long before man, as the first false gods of the earth. Others fell to the sea where they became mermaids, selkies and other water spirits. Others were pure evil and fell to hell, where they are ruled by the devil and tempt humankind with their glamour. They teach witches how to make potions and cast spells. One fairy asked a man if she could be saved and he replied 'Yes, if she could say "our father who art in heaven" but she could only say "our father who wert in heaven" indicating her allegiance to Satan.

In Ireland the monks who collected and wrote down the ancient fairy lore had felt ill at ease with the theological implications of this otherworld of pre-Christian belief. Sometimes they treated the tales as mere stories and on other occasions as ancient history. Gradually, towards the end of the middle ages, the less tolerant belief in the demonic origins of fairies spread to Ireland from continental theologians. A text dating from the early fifteenth century describes fairies as dwellers in mounds and under water and identifies them with the *Tuatha Dé Dannan*. The writer commented: 'Some say that they were demons of a different grade who came with the exiled band of Lucifer from heaven. They assume airy bodies for the purpose of destroying and tempting the descendants of Adam.'

In the Irish folklore of the time God is said to have relented slightly and said: 'where they are, may they stay there.' To fill the places left in heaven by the casting out of the fairies God created the human race. He is said to have given humans red blood to distinguish them from the fairies, whose blood was white. If any whitish liquid was seen on the ground it was subsequently said to be the spilt blood of rival troops of fairies who had fought during the night.

Their white blood prevented fairies from gaining places in heaven. This is said to explain abductions by fairies, as they wish to assimilate and interbreed with humans. The fairy race would thus gain more red blood and be able to enter the kingdom of heaven. Boys were said to be especially at risk of abduction owing to the popular belief that males gave more of their characteristics to any offspring.

Others took a kindlier view. Robert Kirk in his book on fairies [1691][1] said that they were of a middle nature between man and angels, of the nature of a condensed cloud best seen at twilight.

CHAPTER EIGHTEEN

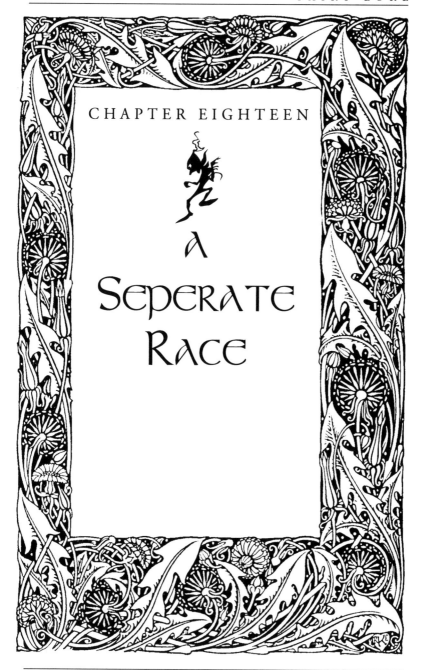

A Seperate Race

Other theorists have proposed that fairies are a folk memory of a forgotten race of human beings. One whimsical hypothesis suggested that they were a tribe of African pygmies that migrated into Europe. Certainly, fairies are often described as being small, and there are many legends of pigmies around the world. The ancient Egyptian pharaoh Assa spoke of seeing a pigmy brought from the land of Punt [Somaliland]. Homer mentioned an annual warfare between pigmies and cranes, probably the origin of the Greek pitikos, miniature fairies who every year are threatened by migrating cranes and have to take arms to drive off the birds from their tiny cattle.

Some authors have claimed that legends of fairies arise when one culture takes over another and drives out the original inhabitants. Merlin Stone[2] suggested that the North German legends of Dark Elves might have arisen from encounters with the original Finnish people who were small and dark. One theory, widely promulgated in the early twentieth century, was that when the Celts invaded Britain and Ireland around 500 BC they drove the natives into wilder and wilder places. Professor Margaret Murray[3] contended that legends of fairies were folk memories of the Neolithic peoples who continued to populate Europe into the Bronze Age. Mediaeval literature described fairies as being small in stature [of the size of twelve-year-old children] and the average height of a Neolithic man was around five feet. Like Neolithic man, fairies were said to have no knowledge of agriculture, but to keep small herds of cattle and subsist on what they could gather or hunt. The tradition that iron gives protection from fairies may have sprung from some dim memory of the Celtic invasions. The Celts were armed with iron, while the race they defeated had weapons of bronze or stone. Elf-bolts, the darts used by fairies and witches to do harm, are actually Stone Age flints. In all areas where pre-Celtic Neolithic monuments, cairns and stone circles exist, they are associated with fairies such as the korreds of Brittany

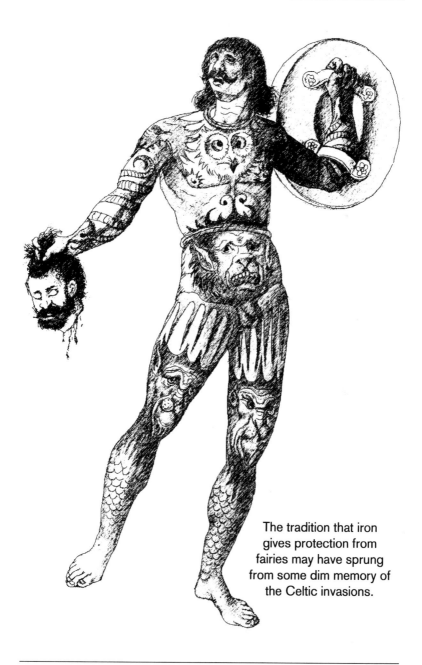

The tradition that iron
gives protection from
fairies may have sprung
from some dim memory of
the Celtic invasions.

and the pyranees of Cornwall who are said to guard them. However, current research suggests that the so-called Celtic invasions may never have taken place on the scale that was previously thought: they may have been cultural offensives rather than physical ones.

Moreover, since fairies are known world wide, this theory of an aboriginal Neolithic race driven to retreat from civilisation and dwell in secret does not stand up to close examination.

Carving of a Woodwose from the church at Peasonhall in Suffolk

Folklorist David MacRitchie went further and argued that fairies derive from distant memories of an earlier race of pre-Neolithic cave dwellers. Forty thousand years ago Cro-Magnon man started to move into a Europe that was still populated by Neanderthals, dark, hairy people with a very different appearance. The Irish legend of the Formorians, a swarthy race described as monstrous

and deformed, whom the Danaans drove out, could possibly describe such an encounter. Ronan Coglan[4] contended that folk memories of Neanderthals may have given rise to legends of satyrs, woodwoses and wildmen, while I.D. Bayanov[5] suggested that they may have contributed to the legends of the rusalka in Eastern Europe.

CHAPTER NINETEEN

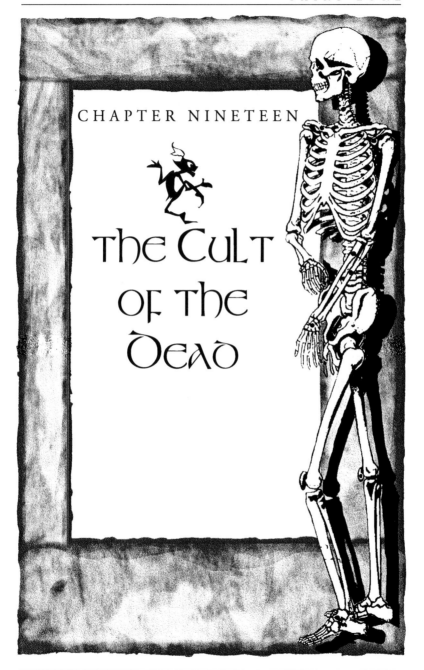

THE CULT OF THE DEAD

Every country in the world has legends of the wandering spirits of the dead, and in many places these have been incorporated into fairy lore. Some tales speak of fairies as the souls of unbaptised children, such as the will o'the wisp, or the Mexican Jimaninos who dance at the Festival of the Dead. The Highland Sluagh are human souls, the hosts of the unforgiven dead, Cornish spriggans are the ghosts of humans and the dunters are the souls of the victims of the Picts. Other stories describe fairies as the souls of Pagans who existed before Christianity or Druids who refused to convert: souls neither good enough for heaven nor evil enough for hell, but expelled to the middle world. The dead were sometimes said to have been captured by fairies and were seen in fairyland or among the fairy hoards, careering about with the Unseelie Court of Scotland or feasting with goblins in churchyards at Halloween. Grant Allen[6] proposed that fairies were the ghosts -or rather folk memories- of the Neolithic dead, as fairies are associated with Neolithic burial mounds throughout Europe.

Some anthropologists regard a belief in fairies as stemming from the Neolithic Cult of the Dead. The dead were buried, often in the foetal position, sometimes in elaborate cairns and mounds, to await a rebirth. The people of the time regarded all life as a cycle- the sun rose [was reborn] each morning, travelled across the sky, sank in the west [died] each evening, travelled through the dark underworld each night and at dawn rose once more. It grew stronger with the summer, weaker with the winter, undergoing a yearly death at the winter solstice before its annual rebirth the next day. The seasons came and went in their turn. Each autumn the seed placed in the earth to return as a new plant in the spring and die with

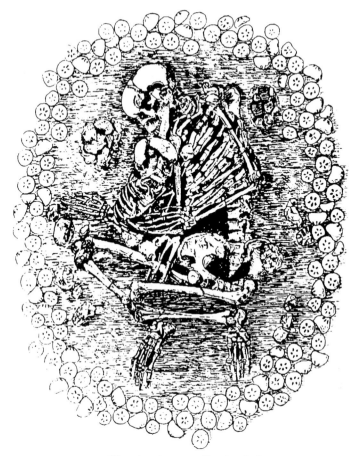

The dead were often buried
in the foetal position to await rebirth

the harvest before the cycle began again. It was reasonable to assume that the same cycle was promised to humankind.

Entrances to fairyland are often said to be through burial mounds and most British, Irish and continental fairies are said to live in the hollow hills in an underground country where the summer never ends. This is comparable with many ancient ideas of the afterlife. The Greeks believed that the souls of the good dwelt in Elysium, which means 'apple-land' or 'apple orchards'. It was a happy realm of perpetual day and the inhabitants could choose to be reborn on earth wherever they elected. The Celts believed that the afterlife was lived in a permanent summer, a land of the ever young; an apple orchard where the trees were always in fruit. In fairy land the passage of time bears no relation to time in the real world as might be expected in a realm inhabited by souls after death.

Newgrange, County Meath

Other fairies lived on magical islands. In European mythology legendary fairy isles of apples are common, and always lie in the west, the place of the dying sun, from which it proceeds to enter the underworld to journey towards its rebirth at dawn. All Neolithic and Bronze Age paradises were orchards; 'paradise' means 'orchard'. The apple was an emblem of the sun- round, changing in colour to red, the colour of the setting sun. The fairies are said to have vanished into the west along the path of the setting sun and fairy islands are often only visible along the path illuminated by the setting sun.

In British tradition the legendary Isle in the West was Avalon, which translates as the 'Isle of Apples', from the Welsh *afal* meaning 'apple'. King Arthur- who was originally a Celtic sun god- was taken there as he lay dying by Morgana ['Of the Sea'], the island spirit who guarded the apples of the Otherworld. Eating a fairy apple confers eternal youth, immortality, or rebirth.

People who are taken to fairyland are warned not eat the food there, or they will never be able to return to the human realms. This echoes ancient Egyptian mythology where the goddess Amenti was associated with the Land of the West, or underworld. She welcomed all deceased people to the land of the dead with bread and water. If they ate and drank they could not return to the land of the living. In Greek myth the goddess of spring Persephone was captured and taken to the underworld where she ate six seeds of a pomegranate. Because of this she was forced to spend six months of each year there, which is why the earth has winter in her absence. In Celtic lore red food was the food of the dead and was forbidden to mankind. The Moari fairies the Patu-paiarehe eat red fruits which are taboo to humans.

The classical Greeks and Romans believed in
nymphs of streams, lakes, and pools.

CHAPTER TWENTY

Nature Spirits

Many early religions were animistic in nature- i.e. a belief that humans, animals, trees, plants, rocks, streams, rivers and certain places have *anima* or soul. As long as certain offerings were made and certain procedures followed, the spirits would remain friendly and beneficent. If they were neglected or offended, they would take their revenge. A river spirit might rise up and drown humans crossing his domain. The spirit of the corn might cause the crops to fail, an apple tree might refuse to be fruitful.

The animistic origins of later Pagan religions can easily be traced. The classical Greeks and Romans believed in dryads and hamadryads as well as nymphs of meadows, mountains, streams, woods, the sea, lakes, pools, and valleys. The Celts and Teutons held trees and groves to be sacred. The ancient Japanese said that trees had souls, especially very old and gnarled trees: the woodcutter saw a spirit in every knotted trunk. The natives of Tasmania believed in demons that resided in trees.

Like the dryads, fairies are often associated with, or thought of living in particular trees. The Albanian Aerico and the Lithuanian Kirnis guard cherry trees. The English Oakmen, the Italian Salvanelli, and the German Wood-wives protect the oak. The ash falls under the safekeeping of the Scandinavian Askafroa, and the Polish Vile. In Ireland the Lunantishee guard the blackthorn, in England and Denmark the Elder Mother safeguards the elder, the Russian Leshiye is associated with the birch and in Czechoslovakia certain fairies take up their abodes in willows. In Africa Huntin lives in the silk cotton tree and Kakua Kambuzi in incense trees. In addition there are a wide variety of fairies that dwell in and watch over trees and forests in general, including the Burmese Nats, the Thai Mother of the Trees, the Buddhist Devas, the Congolese Eloko, the Kulaks of Burma, the Swedish Grove Folk, the Indian Sankchinnis and Vanadevatas, the Scottish Ghillie Dhu and the Siberian elves. The Celts and Teutons imposed the death penalty on people who felled certain trees.

The Celts and other tribes also sacrificed treasure to lakes and river spirits. At the site of Flag Fen in Cambridgeshire over three hundred bronze artefacts were found including pins and ornaments, rings and a large number of weapons including swords and daggers and tools such a chisels and awls [7]. The swords were either unsharpened or broken, and there was a pair of bronze shears, which would have been too soft to cut anything, the shields were too thin to be used, the spears too large. The weapons were obviously ritual ones.

There are large numbers of water fairies around the world including nixies, sirens, undines, mermaids, the fin-folk, selkies, the asrai, banniks, the bisimbi and the bé find. These fairies are temperamental in character and can either curse with storms or drowning or bless with treasure or the power of healing or magic. Some water fairies such as Peg O'Nell of the River Ribble in Lancashire demand sacrifices. She will be satisfied with a small animal or bird but if this is not offered she will take a human life. Tiddy Mun had to be placated when the Fens were drained.

Amongst the Arthurian legends is the tale of Vivienne, the Lady of the Lake. She was a beautiful fairy who snatched the baby Lancelot from his real mother and disappeared with him into the depths of a lake, where she tenderly brought him up in an underwater kingdom, preparing him for greatness. She also supplied Arthur with his magical sword Excaliber, a gift from the land of the fairy, whose sheath safeguarded its owner from harm. She may have been one of the Welsh Gwragedd Annwn. Elisabeth Oakland suggested that perhaps divine kingship was a gift of the fairy[8].

In Latin, the term *genius* is applied to spirit which rules over a person, place or nation. The word is often used to denote the spirit of the forest, who exists in various forms world-wide. His voice is heard in the breeze or in the rustle of leaves. In some European countries he is depicted carrying an uprooted pine tree. A Genius Loci is the guardian spirit of a particular place. Many fairies are described as protecting particular localities such as certain groves, ancient sites and bridges. These fairies are often described as 'white ladies' and there are many of them throughout the world from the African Shamantin to the Irish banshees. In Normandy they are the fairies of ravines, fords, bridges, and other narrow places. A white lady appears in the Arthurian myths: Guinevere means 'white phantom', which indicates that she may have been of fairy origin, the guardian spirit of a place, maybe Albion itself. Perhaps if Guinevere was the guardian spirit of Albion, Morgan le Fay was the *Mor Gwyn* ['white lady'] of the Otherworld, Avalon, the magical island outside time and space where illness, old age and death were unknown. The island was covered in apple orchards and inhabited by nine sisters of which Morgan was the most beautiful and most powerful. She had knowledge of shapeshifting and could turn herself into any animal or bird, and knew the properties of all plants for healing and magic. As Arthur lay dying after the battle of Camlann Morgan appeared with a ship of women and carried him to Avalon.

Many fairies are associated with vegetation, crops, and the fertility of the land, with the power of either blessing or blighting. They are capable of stealing the spirit of the land, so that ears would not ripen on the corn, or cattle fatten. These fairies may be directly related to vegetation spirits. The German Kornbôcke causes the crops to ripen. The Russian Polevik grows with the corn and after the harvest shrinks to the size of the stubble. The Russian Rusalky caused the corn to grow when they moved through it.

In England there is a saying that 'the little elves fly away on the brown oak leaves' meaning that they disappear for the winter, like the vegetation spirits. Elves and fairies were both thought to be happy to take part in human family gatherings at Christmas, and greenery was hung at that festival so that the elves could take shelter in it from the wintry weather. This may be directly descended from the Druidic custom of hanging up evergreens in the winter as shelter for the vegetation spirits during the dead time of the year. Green men, wood woses etc. were once vegetation spirits, and many fairies are said to either have green skin or to dress in green, which many people still call the fairy colour and claim is unlucky for humans to wear. There are various stories of green children which have been discovered on hillsides or at cave mouths during the centuries, and the finders often concluded that they were fairy children which had strayed from fairy realms beneath the earth. Most fairies haunt wild places, especially ancient woodlands and forests, which they protect. Often it is dangerous for human beings to enter these places and they will be attacked by fairies or pixie led [led astray]. Puck and Robin Goodfellow play tricks on those who enter their domain.

Some fairies protect animals or are part animal themselves, most commonly possessing small horns and the legs and feet of goats or deer like the Greek and Roman nature gods Pan and Faunus and the nature spirits the satyrs and fauns. Robin Goodfellow has horns and goat feet as does the Slavic Catez, and both may be later incarnations of horned spirits of the wild such as the Celtic Cernunnos. Many fairies can appear as animals when they chose, especially horses and dogs.

Other fairies seem to represent spirits of weather- wind, storm, rain, lightening, sunshine and so on. The Wind Knots or Folletti of Italy ride storms, the Guriuz bring good weather to farmers, Munya is the lightening while her brothers are the two thunders, the salvanelli raise storms to ride on the wind and the Swedish Skosrâ is a violent whirlwind. Some fairies bring about the change of seasons, such as the Russian Father Frost and the Scottish Cailleach who bring winter. While good fairies like Robin Goodfellow are said to be active during the summer months, evil fairies like the Phooka are most active during the winter months, suggesting that they may once have represented the opposing powers of growth and blight. A Bulgarian song tells how, without

a touch of wind, the forest was uprooted by the mere touch of dragons with long white hair as they passed over the forest in gold chariots, accompanied by their wives, and their children in cradles of gold. The dragons perhaps represent the snowy winter, their wives the days of summer which they carry away, and the children the days of springtime, which they will bring back.

The Theosophical Society, an occult group founded in the nineteenth century, believe that nature fairies or devas live in a hidden spiritual realm that co-exists with our own. Devas' bodies consist of the very finest of physical matter but they can manifest on the etheric level as animals, plants and people, reflecting the preconceptions of the observer. The energy flowing through them is often interpreted as hair and wings, though their normal state is a pulsating sphere of light with a bright nucleus. Their function is to absorb energy from the sun and distribute this to the physical world, playing an important role in the spiritual aspects of photosynthesis. Modern occultists refer to devas as 'The Middle Kingdom' or 'The Lordly Ones'. In the 1970s the Findhorn settlers in the north of Scotland claimed to have appealed to plant devas to help them grow vegetables on very poor soil with astounding results.

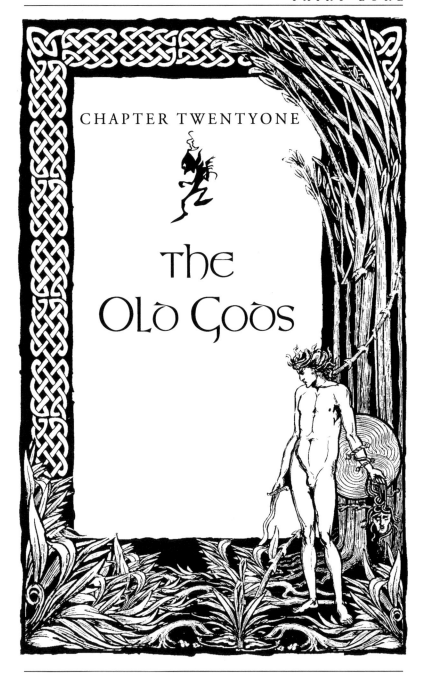

CHAPTER TWENTYONE

THE OLD GODS

Religions change and evolve; modifying old concepts and embracing new ideas as contacts with other cultures are made. It is difficult to draw a line and say where the old animistic nature spirits end and gods and goddesses begin. Many Pagan deities are anthropomorphic representations of nature or the heavens- the sun, moon, stars, sky, corn, earth, weather, seasons etc. Later deities also embody such abstract principles as love, war, poetry and art.

It can be no coincidence that the festivals most associated with fairies are the four fire festivals of the Celts and the solstices and equinoxes almost universally celebrated by Pagans.

Samhain [Halloween] marked the start of winter, and the ancient Celts celebrated it as a festival of the dead. In fairy lore good fairies such as the Tuatha de Danaan and the English Puck retire from sight after Samhain until spring returns. Evil fairies, such as the Scottish Unseelie Court, become very active, goblins are seen consorting with ghosts, and evil omens such as black fairy dogs and the Bean-nighe or Washer at the Ford appear. Fairy mounds open at Hollantide and the Hogmen, the most feared of the Manx fairies, move their abode. After Halloween, all the crops left unharvested belong to the fairies. In Ireland, Halloween is called Phooka Night and after this time he renders all the crops unfit to eat and spoils all the blackberries. In Wales gryphons perform the same offices. The Lunatishee will not allow blackthorn to be cut on November 11th [old Samhain]

Seasonal winter/death goddesses may be discerned in various hag fairies like the Cailleach Beinne Bhic Horo who cares for red deer [the Celtic totem animal for Samhain], the Cailleach Bleur who beats down vegetation and Frau Holda who brings the snow.

At Yule, particularly in Scandinavian and Germanic countries, a wide variety of present giving fairies appear. The Icelandic Jola Sveinar, the Danish Julenisse, the Swedish Jultomte and of course Father Christmas deliver gifts. These are probably directly descended from Odin or Woden who rode out at Yule to reward good deeds and punish bad ones.

Good fairies are most active from Beltane [May Day] to Samhain echoing the ancient return of the gods of summer and increase. The Cailleach Bheur gives up her struggle and allows summer to chase away winter. In Leicestershire, the Black Annis hunt was held every May Day to chase the summer hare. In Arthurian legend Guinevere, thought by many to be of fairy origin, rode out a maying, dressed in fairy

green. The Lunatishee, the Irish Blackthorn Fairies, guard the sacred thorn and will not allow it to be cut on May 11th [old Beltane].

One of the great fairy festivals is midsummer, the ancient celebration of the summer solstice and the sun god. At this time they are said to have their greatest power and be at their most frolicsome. The Irish spirit the Amadan-na-Briona at his most active, playing mischievous tricks on people. The fairies try to pass around the Baal fires in a whirlwind to extinguish them. Humans can protect themselves by leaping through the fire and their cattle by driving them through the embers, passing glowing coals three times over and three times under the body of each animal, an ancient method of ritual purification.

The various brownie [or home sprite] type fairies around the world, such as the Spanish Ancho, the Polynesian Atua, the Russian Bagan, the Irish bean-tighe, the Scots bodachan sabhaill, the Welsh bwbach and bwca, the Japanese Chin-chin Kobakama and the Chinese Choa Phum Phi, are similar in character to the Roman Lars Familiaris, household gods which guarded each family.

When Christianity spread across Europe, the old gods were either designated Christian saints [the Goddess Brighid, for example, became St Brigit] or entirely demonised. However, recollections of the old gods probably persisted among the ordinary people as spirits that were occasionally seen and still had to be honoured less they should be angered. It may be that the old gods eventually passed into folk memory as lesser spirits or fairies. This theory is most clearly illustrated by the legend of the Tuatha de Danaan ['People of the Goddess Danu'] who were said to be a race of gods who landed in Ireland one Beltane and drove back the Firbolg to take possession of the island. They were tall and fair and had many talents. When they were eventually conquered in turn by the Celts they dwindled in size and retreated to the hollow hills or beneath the lakes of Ireland becoming the Daoine Sidhe or 'People of the Hills'. In many places until quite recent times offerings of milk were poured onto mounds or the standing stones the old gods were said to have built. Some of the baking and the harvest had to be left for the 'fairies' and various precautions taken so as not to offend them.

A large number of named fairies are directly traceable to specific old gods. Leicestershire's Black Annis was once the goddess Anu, the sea fairies the Shoneys are descended from the Norse sea goddess Sjofn, the Romanian fairy Ileana was once a goddess of the dawn, Aine was a goddess of the Tuatha de Danaan, Gwydion, who rules the Tylwyth Teg, was once a Celtic god. There are literally thousands of examples.

The word fairy is derived from the Latin *fata* ['fate'], via the Old French *faerie*. In Greek myth the Three Fates appear, always clothed in white. They control human destiny. Their Greek name means 'phase' as in the phases of the moon and they are in fact the triple moon goddess, the spinner and measurer of time. The thread of life is spun on Clotho's spindle, measured by the rod of Lachesis and snipped by Atropos' shears. In stature Atropos is the smallest of the three, but by far the most feared, relating as she does to the hag of winter, the waning or dark moon and the death goddess. An amazing number of fairies are associated with spinning and flax. The circular action of the spinning wheel is associated with the turning of the zodiac through the heavens, the turning of day and night, the passage of the seasons and the cycle of life itself. The movement of the spindle, both back and forth and in a circular motion, is sometimes seen as an image of the cosmos, making the continuos thread of life. For this reason the flax is sacred to the Weaver Goddess, who spins the thread of life and weaves the fabric of the cosmos, the warp and weft of fate.

The Weaver Goddess appears in many mythologies in various forms. The Three Fates of Greek myth are paralleled in Norse lore by the Three Norns, Urd, Verdani and Skuld, who weave the web of fate and are another representation of the Triple Moon Goddess. Arianrhod is the Welsh weaver goddess. Her name means 'silver wheel', which is the spinning wheel of the moon and the stars. She is mistress of Caer Arianrhod, situated in the Corona Borealis. It is the Spiral Castle to which the soul journeys at death, following the spiralling thread, and where initiation and rebirth takes place.

Like fairies, the weaver goddess is always associated with magic. The Egyptian Isis was the patroness of weaving but she also wove magic and could heal, as all fairies and witches are said to be able to do. The Egyptian goddess Meith was also known as a magician and her symbol was a weaver's shuttle. She was titled 'The Opener of the Ways' and conducted souls to the underworld. This idea of following a linen thread into or out of the underworld is echoed in other cultures, Ariadne lead Theseus out of the underworld maze of the Minotaur by means of a thread, while the witch goddess Hecate lead the corn goddess Demeter into the underworld with a thread to find her daughter Persephone [Spring].

The underworld is reputed to be where the fairies live, and many of them, like leprechauns and dragons, guard treasure. If the fairies are really the old gods, the treasures they guard are the secrets of the Goddess: her cauldron of renewal and rebirth.

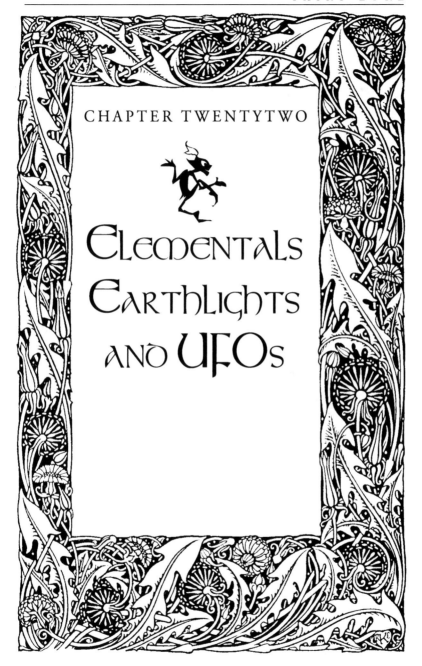

CHAPTER TWENTYTWO

Elementals
Earthlights
and UFOs

Elementals

Some occultists believe that fairies are elementals- creatures of earth, air, fire or water. Aristotle thought that everything was composed of a combination of these four elements, an idea that persisted in scientific thought until the seventeenth century. They are the first growth of primal matter and each composed two of the four primal humours- hot, cold, wet and dry. Fire was hot and dry, water cold and wet and so on. The powers of the spirits of the elements are called on by magicians who maintain that they are beings who evolved along another line to humans. In the Cabala they are called the Shedim.

The elemental spirits were of great interest to the alchemists. According to the alchemist, doctor and philosopher Paracelsus [1493-1541] in his 'Treatise on Elemental Sprites' the earth elementals were pygmies or gnomi [singular gnomus] who could move through the earth as fish move through water. The derivation of the word is uncertain, but may relate to the Greek verb 'to know' or yet again to 'of the earth'. Though the concept of gnomes does not seem to pre-date Paracelsus [though the idea of earth spirits does] gnomes have captured the popular imagination as guardians of the earth. He called spirits of the air sylphs from the Greek silphe meaning 'butterfly' or 'moth'. They are described as almost transparent, very small and winged. Salamanders [from the Greek meaning 'fireplace'] were designated elemental spirits of the fire. They are usually portrayed as the lizards of the same name. Undines ['Wave'] are regarded as representing water.

Earthlights

Will o'the wisps and other such fairies have been explained away as rotting vegetation giving rise to gasses such as methane which ignite to form flames and fire balls which are then blown about on the breeze. Scientists have in recent years disputed the fact that this could happen at all. Dr Alan Mills[9] at Leicester University's Department of Geology tried to duplicate will o the wisp type fires but found he could not, nor could he find any natural spark that would ignite the gasses. Such flames would hardly move about and seem to dance as will o'the wisps have been witnessed to do. Despite this such lights continue to appear.

One explanation of will o'the wisp type fairies current among earth mysteries experts like Paul Devereux[10] is that they are earthlights, electrical charges built up in areas of geological stress and slowly discharged as electrons into the air. It is demonstrable that tectonic strain in rocks- especially those near geological fault

lines- can cause anomalous light phenomena. Such earthlights have been witnessed in both Britain and Japan before earthquakes. According to David Clarke[11] the Celtic countries of Ireland, Scotland and Wales have a tradition of corpse candles or fairy lanterns appearing as an omen of death. Lights in pit tunnels have warned of impending disasters and haunt mines where catastrophes have claimed lives.

Many of the ancient sites traditionally associated with fairies are reputed to be focal points of 'earth energy' and centres of healing and earthlight activity. In 1978 Deveraux launched the 'Dragon Project' (named after the Chinese ideogram which represents terrestrial energy currents). Based at the Rollright Stones in

Oxfordshire, the research carried out used scientific technology and psychic methods such as dowsing to investigate the site. Geiger counter readings showed slightly higher radiation counts within the circle, recalling the discovery of uranium deposits on Native American and Australian sacred land. Megalith builders may have been attracted to naturally radioactive sites without knowing why. Magnetometer readings showed a high magnetic field with rapid fluctuations at one particular stone. This may give credence to folk beliefs about the healing properties of megaliths for the cure of broken bones, as modern medicine has discovered that electromagnetism speeds up the healing of fractures. Strange energy readings, identified as ultrasound beyond the range of human hearing, were detected, usually beginning just before sunrise and ending one or two hours later. 'The stones have begun to reveal some of their secrets,' says Devereux 'We have much left to learn'.

Devereux has speculated that earthlights may generate enough energy to cause temporal lobe stimulation, which causes visual hallucinations. Subjects have also reported other such as people pulling at their limbs or a sequence of events that resemble accounts of alien abductions[12].

UFOs

Accounts of people kidnapped by fairies and taken to the hollow hills resemble recent literature on alien abductions[22]. The themes of amnesia, time loss, lampless lights and seduction are common to both experiences. Perhaps it is a sign of the age that what was once put down to devils, witches and fairies is now often put down to aliens and UFOs.

There are many links between fairies and mushrooms.
A number of legends speak of one eyed, one legged creatures,
and these may, in fact, be a code for psychotropic mushrooms.

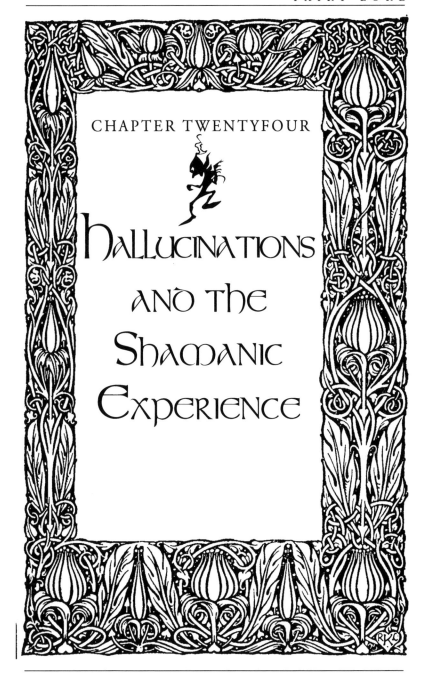

CHAPTER TWENTYFOUR

Hallucinations and the Shamanic Experience

There are many links between fairies and mushrooms. The magical rings where they dance are circles of mushrooms. English oakmen offer food to passing mortals that turns out to be poisonous fungi disguised by magic. The Swedish para can be made to appear by taking a certain mushroom, frying it in tar, salt and sulphur and beating it with a rod. Fairies are commonly depicted sitting on top of the red and white spotted mushroom, fly agaric [*Amanita muscaria*] and they commonly also wear red hats.

Fly agaric is psychotropic and has a long history of use among European mystics and shamans. In Finno-Ugric languages words denoting ecstasy and intoxication are traceable to root expressions meaning 'fly agaric'. The effects of the mushroom include auditory and visual hallucinations and spatial distortions. Subjects commonly report sensations of flying, or seeing little people or red-hatted mushrooms dancing. Fly agaric grows under birch trees and the Siberian shaman's seven-stepped pole was made of birch. In other words, the shaman ingested the mushroom and flew up the *axis mundi* tree to the spirit realms, seeing the tutelary spirit of the agaric as a red-capped fairy.

The Father Christmas costume of white and red also suggests the mushroom. Siberian winter dwellings were excavated holes with a birch log roofs; the only entrance was through a smoke hole in the roof. Even the summer dwellings had smoke-hole exits for the spirit of the shaman to fly out of when he was in a trance. This might explain why Santa enters and exits through the chimney. Why does Santa bring gifts? The shaman is the middleman between humans and spirits and brings back knowledge from the spirit world. Ordinary individuals would write requests on pieces of paper and burn, so their messages would be carried to the spirits on the smoke.

The Rig-Veda speaks of the mysterious soma, a plant that was considered a god: an aspect of Agni, the god of fire. The plant had no roots, leaves, blossoms or seeds but possessed of a single eye like the sun- the red cap of the fly agaric[13]. Spoken of as an eye, the cap of the fly agaric represents the opening of inner vision, as well as the sun.

A number of legends speak of one eyed, one legged creatures, and these may, in fact, be a code for psychotropic mushrooms[14]. The fachan, a Highland fairy, has one eye, one hand, one leg, one ear, one arm and one toe all lined up down the centre of his body. He carries a spiked club with which he attacks any human who dares to approach his mountain realm. He hates all living creatures but especially birds, which he envies for their gift of flight. A number of writers have theorised that the fachan may be a folk memory of the Celtic shamans, who stood on one leg and closed one eye when casting spells. The usual explanation offered for this practice is so that one eye looks into the inner realms, and only standing on one leg symbolises not being wholly in one realm or another[15]. However, it may be that the stance is in imitation of the mushroom that gives the shaman his power, the one-legged, one-eyed fly agaric. The fact that the fachan inhabits a mountainous region is significant, as that is where the fly agaric grows. His hatred of birds, which he envies for their flight, may be a distorted folk memory of the gift of flight the mushroom bestows.

There was also an Irish race of one-legged, one-eyed beings[16] described as the oldest inhabitants of the land, a race of wizards who intermarried with the Tuatha de Danaan. In Celtic lore all red food was taboo, including rowan berries and red nuts. Peter Lamborn Wilson[17] has suggested that these may be masks for the mushroom in Irish myth, adding that the Celts were head hunters, believing that all wisdom and power resided in the head.

Perhaps these heads were not only human ones but also the heads of vision giving mushrooms. Mushrooms appear in Greek mythology in connection with the sun god Apollo. Carl Ruck[18] speculated that the votive offerings sent to Apollo's shrine at Delos from Hyperborea [sometimes identified with Siberia] were actually fly agaric mushrooms. Along the route the offerings travelled lived a race called the Arimaspeans ['One-eyed']. The murder of the Cyclops ['Round-eye'] occasioned Apollo's sojourn amongst the peoples of his northern homeland, Hyperborea. There was also a race of one-footed creatures called Shade-foots who, according to Aristophanes, were implicated in a profane celebration of the lesser Eleusinian mysteries. The Shade foots were also known as Monocoli ['One-legs']. In Vedic Sanskrit soma is described as 'Not-born Single-foot'.

Fairy food, which is generally described as being red in colour, is prohibited for humans. Should they eat it, they can never return to the realm of men. This is comparable with the taboos placed on shamanic substances forbidding them to ordinary men and women. Among the Selkup fly agaric was believed to be fatal to non shamans. Among the Vogul consumption was limited to sacred occasions and it was abused on peril of death. The Indo Europeans strictly limited the important ritual of soma to certain classes and the profane user risked death at the hands of the angry god. Amongst the Celts, red foods and mushrooms were taboo, designated as the food of the otherworld or the dead. As the mushroom aids the shaman to visit other realms in spirit flight, see spirits and contact the spirit or god within, Robert Graves[19] argued that ambrosia, the food of the gods, was in reality hallucinogenic mushrooms.

Descriptions of visits to fairyland might easily describe a drug induced visionary experience-enhanced colours, unearthly music, spatial distortions, the loss of any sense of the passage of time, and food and drink tasting wonderful. The Rig-veda states 'I am huge, huge! Flying to the cloud. Have I not drunk soma?' However, when the traveller returns [or the vision ends] fairy gold turns to withered leaves or common rubbish.

Fly agaric is only one of a number of psychoactive drugs used by shamans which generate sensations of flying, visions and perceptual enhancement. Kevin Callahan documented the experience of Ojibwa Indians who saw little people for about thirty minutes during hallucinations induced by Atropine plants from the Deadly Nightshade family[20]. Even alcohol withdrawal has been known to induce fancies of little people[21].

Fairies are said to dwell in mounds, caves or underground in general and a common shamanic experience is the visit to the underworld. Shamans and witches are said to receive their powers of spirits or fairies. Fairies can confer gifts of healing and magic and prophecy.

Fairy animals often appear to signal the beginning of a spiritual quest. Fairies are said to ride horses, or turn into them to trick the unwary into mounting them and then taking off on a wild ride. Gods and shamen tether their horses to the

World Tree, the *axis mundi* via which journeys to all the realms is possible. The horse spirit carries the shaman into other worlds. A shaman's drum is often referred to as his 'horse', since the drumbeat is a vehicle that enables him to travel to other realms. The Irish horse Aonbharr carried the hero Conan to the Otherworld. Thomas the Rhymer was taken to the realm of the fairy by the milk white steed of the elf queen, and Tam Lin escaped from the fairy realm on a stolen white horse.

In Greek myth the horse of Otherworld journeying was Pegasos [Latin Pegasus] who was the horse of Apollo, the Muses and the inspiration of poetry. On Helicon there was a spring called Hippocrene ['the horse well'] which was horse-shoe shaped and was said to have been made when Pegasus ['of the springs of water'] stamped there; poets drank its waters for inspiration. If a poet said 'I am mounting my Pegasus' he meant that he was inspired to write poetry. Poetry and bardship was a serious business, not mere rhyme making, it meant being touched by the gods and being given divine inspiration from the other realms. Many famous poets and musicians are said to have learned their craft in the Otherworld or the realm of the fairy.

1 Kirk, Robert, The Secret Commonwealth 1691

2 Stone, Merlin, Ancient Mirrors of Womanhood

3 Murray, Margaret, The God of the Witches, Faber and Faber 1931

4 Coglan, Ronan, Handbook of Fairies, Capall Bann 1998

5 Bayanov, I.D., In the Steps of the Russian Snowman, Moscow 1996

6 Allen, Grant, Cornhill Magazine No. 43, 1881

7 Pearce, Marion K., 'Flag Fen Lake Village',
Silver Wheel February 1997

8 Oakland Elisabeth 'Lost in Faery', At the Edge No 10 June 1998

9 Mills, A.A. 'Will o'the Wisp', Chemistry in Britain No 16 1980

10 Devereux, Paul, Earth Lights Revelation-
UFOs and mystery lightform phenomena, Blandford 1989

11 Clarke, David, 'Peakland Spooklights',
At The Edge No 10, June 1998

12 Trubshaw, Bob, Fairies and Their Kin,
At the Edge no 10, June 1998

13 Wasson, Gordon, Soma: The Divine Mushroom of Immortality,
Harcourt Brace Jovanovick Inc, 1968

14 Wasson, Gordon, Soma: The Divine Mushroom of Immortality,
Harcourt Brace Jovanovick Inc, 1968

15 Matthews, John, Taliesin, The Aquarian Press 1991

16 Wilson, Peter Lamborn, Irish Soma,
http://www.lycaeum.org/~lux/features/irshsoma.htm]

17 Wilson, Peter Lamborn, Irish Soma,
http://www.lycaeum.org/~lux/features/irshsoma.htm]

18 Ruck, Carl, The Offerings from the Hyperboreans,
Persephone's Quest, Yale, New Haven, 1986

19 Graves, Robert, The White Goddess, Faber and Faber, 1961

20 Callahan, Kevin, Rock Art and Lilliputian Hallucinations,
www.geocities.com/Athens /2996/trace2b.html#lil

21 Trubshaw, Bob, 'Fairies and Their Kin',
At the Edge No 10, June 1998

22 Bord, Janet, Fairies- Real Encounters With Little People,
Michael O'Mara, 1997

INDEX

Abatwa 126
Abduction 84, 131
Aerico 144
Afal 56
Afterlife 140
Aine 92, 155
Air 158
Alder 50
Alexander the Great 89
Alfar 3
Alien abductions 161
Alnus glutinosa 50
Alvgest 32
Amadan-na-Briona 118
Amalthea 71
Amanita muscaria 46, 164
Amenti 141
Ancho 154
Ancient sites 146, 160
Angels, fallen 130
Anglo Saxon 40
Anima 144
Animistic 144, 152
Anthropomorphic representations
    152
Ants 126
Anu 155
Aonbharr 168
Apollo 64, 166
Apple 56
Apple Tree Man 119
Apple-land 140
Ariadne 156
Arianrhod 156
Arimaspeans 166
Aristophanes 166

Arrowheads 30
Artemis 64
Arthurian legend
Arthurian myths & legends
    117, 146, 147, 153
Askafroa 144
Asrai 145
Atropine 167
Atropos 155
Atua 154
Autumn Equinox 119
Avalon 19, 141, 147
Axis mundi 168

Baal 154
Baby 77
Bac 18
Bagan 154
Bakhna Rakhna 126
Baking 40, 108
Banniks 145
Banshees 6, 147
Bardship 168
Bast 60
Bastet 60
Bat 70
Bé find 145
Bean-nighe 152
Bean-tighe 154
Bear 99
Beaumont, John 7
Befana 120
Bells 39
Beltane 117, 153
Berchte 120
Bergfolk 110

Betula alba 54
Bible 38
Bile ratha 47
Birch 54
Bisimbi 145
Black Annis 74, 117, 153, 155
Blackberry 56
Blackthorn 55
Blackthorn Fairies 117
Blake, William 4
Blood 91
Blood, white 131
Blue Hag of Winter 60
Bluebell 50
Boar 63
Bodachan sabhaill 154
Bran 20, 66
Bratach Sith 108
Breton fairies 110
Bridges 147
Brighid 60, 154
Bright one 120
Bristol Channel 22
Bronze Age 134, 140
Brownie 154
Burial mounds 139
Burton, Captain George 108
Butterflies 124
Butterfly 60, 159
Bwbach 154

Cabala 158
Caer Arianrhod 156
Caibe sith 31
Cailleach Beinne Bhic Horo 153
Cailleach Bheur 61, 117
Cailleach Bleur 153
Cait sith 60
Callicantzaroi 120

Calluna vulgaris 48
Campbell, Gregory John 127
Capricorn 72
Cat 60, 105
Caterpillars 124
Cattle 61
Cauldron 108
Ceaird chomuinn 108
Celtic shamans 165
Celtic sun god 141
Celts 140, 144, 152, 154, 166
Céol-Sidhe 102
Ceridwen 61
Cernunnos 66, 148
Changeling 76, 77
Channel Isles 19
Child, dead 79
Children, stolen 79
Children, unbaptised 81
Chillingham Castle 62
Choa Phum Phi 154
Christian doctrine 130
Christian saints 154
Christian symbols 38
Christianity 138
Christmas 120
Church Folk 110
Churn-milk Peg 47
Clothes 37
Clotho 155
Cnoc 18
Conan 168
Corn dolly 41
Corona Borealis 156
Corpse candles 160
Corylus avellana 47
Count Raymond 93
Cowslip 52
Cramps 32

Crataegus monogyna 52
Cro sith 61
Cro-Magnon man 136
Cu sith 66
Cuckoo 65
Cycle of life 155
Cyclops 166

Daemonologie 130
Daoine Beaga 3
Daoine Coire 3
Daoine Matha 3
Daoine Sidhe 3, 127, 154
Dark Elves 134
Dark God 68
Dead 138
Dead, cult of 138
Deadly Nightshade 167
Dealan-de 60
Dearbadan-de 60
Deer 65, 148
Deformities 32
Demeter 156
Demon 130
Devas 144, 149
Diana 60
Diarmuid 64
Digitalis purpurea 45
Dog 66, 105
Dracae 111
Dragon Project 160
Druidic custom 147
Druids 138
Dryads 144
Dunvegan Castle 108

Each sith 69
Eagle 72
Earl of Desmond 92

Earl of Fitzgerald 92
Earth 158
Earthlights 159
Echinite 32
Eggshell 78
Egyptian mythology 141
Einherier 67
Elder 44
Elder Mother 144
Elementals 158
Eleusinian mysteries 166
Elf-arrows 30
Elf-bolts 30, 122, 134
Elf-shot 30
Elf-stroke 30
Elinas 93
Eloko 144
Elves 147
Elysium 57, 140
Emain Ablach 20
Equinoxes 152
Eudamarac 90
Excaliber 146

Fachan 165
Fairies, Victorian view of 6
Fairy animals 167
Fairy Banner 108
Fairy Boy of Leith 108
Fairy bride 88
Fairy colour 148
Fairy food 166
Fairy gifts 108
Fairy gold 110
Fairy lanterns 160
Fairy loves 88
Fairy mounds 152
Fairy music 102
Fairy Queen 99

Fairy Rade 9
Fairy Ring Mushrooms 47
Fairyland 139
Fairyland, visits to 98
Fatare 3
Father Christmas 120, 164
Father Frost 120, 148
Faunus 148
Fern 53
Fertility 68, 147
Festival of the Dead 119, 138
Festivals 116
Fiddler 104
Fin MacCool 20
Fin-folk 145
Findhorn 127, 150
Firbolg 154
Fire 42, 158
Fire balls 159
Fire festivals 152
Flint 30
Fly agaric 46, 164-167
Folk memories 138
Folletti 148
Formorians 72, 136
Forts 17
Fortunate Islands 21
Fountauin of Thirst 94
Four leafed clover 52
Fox 105
Foxglove 45, 77
Frau Holda 120
Frensham 108
Freya 60
Fridays 116
Frog 68
Fuil siochaire 31
Fungi 57, 164

Garbh Ogh 50
Geiger counter 161
Genius Loci 146
Ghillie Dhu 144
Ghosts 119, 138
Glamour 99
Glastonbury 19
Goat 71, 105, 148
Goblins 119, 138, 152
Goddess of spring 141
Gods and goddesses 152
Gold 16, 108
Good People 126
Goshawk 90
Gowdie, Isobel 122
Graves, Robert 167
Greek myth 141
Greeks 71, 144
Green Meadows of Enchantment
    22
Green men 148
Griffiths, Frances 127
Ground ivy 41
Grove Folk 144
Groves 146
Gryphons 120, 153
Gwartheg y Llyn 63
Gwerddonau Llion 22
Gwragedd Annwn 146
Gwyn ap Nudd 67

Hag-ridden 55
Halfdane, Isobel 122
Halloween 117, 119, 138, 152
Hallucinations 164
Hamadryads 144
Hare 74
Harvest Home 119
Harvest maiden 41

Hawthorn 52
Hazel 47
Hazel Nut Fairies 119
Head hunters 166
Healing 108, 145
Heather 26, 48
Heaven 130, 131
Heavens 152, 155
Hecate 156
Henwen 64
Herlathing 67
Herne the Hunter 66
Highland Sluagh 138
Hillmen 119
Hippocrene 168
Hogmen 119, 152
Hollantide 119, 152
Hollow hills 16, 154
Horned spirits 148
Horse 69, 168
Horseshoe 37
Huntin 144
Hy-Breasail 20
Hyacinthoides non-scriptus 50

Ileana 155
Immortality 141
Impetigo 32
Iron 37, 134
Iron bar 99
Iron implements 78
Isis 156
Isle in the West 141
Isle of Glass 23
Isle of Man 20
Isles of the Blest 21

Jeffries, Anne 123
Jimaninos 119

Jola Sveinar 120
Jubuk 120
Julenisse 120
Jultomte 120

Kakua Kambuzi 144
Keightley , Thomas 127
Kermode, T.C. 7
Kine of the Lake 63
King Ancaeus 64
King Arthur 56, 72, 141
King Finvarra 103
King Gavran 22
King Harald Hardrada 109
King James I 130
King of Albania 93
King of the Cats 61
King Sil 16
Kingship, divine 146
Kirk, Robert 132
Kirkonwaki 110
Kirnis 144
Kornbocke 118
Kornbôcke 147
Korreds 110
Kugarvad 61
Kulaks 144

Lachesis 155
Lady of the Lake 146
Lady Wilde 127
Lammas marks 118
Lancelot 146
Land of the Fairies 94
Land of the West 141
Land of Youth 22
Lars Familiaris 154
Launfal 89
Lay D'Ywenec 90

Leprechaun 72, 111
Leshiye 144
Little people 167
Llyn Dan Ychen 62
Llyn y Fan Fach 95
Lochlann 22
Londonderry Air 105
Lordly Ones 150
Lough Neagh 20
Lucifer 131
Lughnasa 118
Lunantishee 117, 144, 153
Lust 68

Mabinogion 68
Mabon 72
MacCrimmons 102
MacLeods of Skye 108
Magic 108, 145
Magical islands 140, 147
Magical powers 122
Magnetic field 161
Malus sp. 56
Manannan 20, 68
Manx fairies 119
Marasmius oreades 47
Marvan 64
May Day 117, 153
Mediaeval literature 134
Megaliths 161
Meith 156
Melch Dick 47
Melior 93
Melusina 93
Merlin 89
Mermaids 145
Middle Kingdom 150
Midsummer Eve 118
Midsummer Night's Dream 48

Milk 122
Minotaur 156
Mirrors 39
Moari fairies 141
Monocoli 166
Mor Gwyn 147
Morgan le Fay 19, 147
Morgana 57, 141
Morris Men 39
Moth 159
Mother of the Trees 144
Mukka Slangha 64
Mulberry 41
Muryans 126
Mushroom 164, 165, 166
Mushroom, hallucinogenic 55
Music 108

Nats 144
Nature gods 148
Nature spirits 144
Neolithic 140
Neolithic peoples 134
New Year 120
Newgrange 65, 140
Niamh 22
Nixies 145
Nymphs 144

Oak 54
Oakmen 54, 144, 164
Oatmeal 39
Oberon 48
Occultists 150
Odin 67, 153
Ogham 55
Oisin 22
Oiteag sluaigh 85
Ojibwa Indian 167

Old gods 154
One-eyed 165, 166
Opener of the Ways 156
Osiris 64
Ostara 117
Othan 18
Otherworld 147, 168

Pagan 144
Pagan deities 152
Pagan symbol 38
Pagans 138
Palatina 93
Pan 71, 148
Pandaemonium 108
Paracelsus 159
Paradise 140
Paralysis 32
Patu-paiarehe 141
Pearlwort 40
Peg O'Nell 145
Pegasos 168
Penelop 94
People of the Hills 127, 155
Persephone 27, 141, 156
Pharaoh 134
Phooka 148
Phooka Night 120, 153
Photographs 127
Phragmites communis 45
Picts 138
Pig 68
Pilwiz 118
Plentyn-newid 76
Poetry 168
Polevik 118, 147
Pookha 67
Potentilla anserina 50
Pouquelaie 19

Pre-Celtic Neolithic monuments
    134
Pre-Christian belief 131
Pretty Girl Milking the Cow 105
Primal humours 158
Primal matter 158
Primrose 51
Primula veris 52
Primula vulgaris 51
Prophecy 108
Prunus spinosa 55
Pryderi 64
Psychotropic 164
Psychotropic mushrooms 165
Puck 48, 67, 148, 152
Pygmies 134

Queen Guinevere 89, 117, 153
Queen of Sheba 89
Quercus robur 54

Race, aboriginal 136
Race, forgotten 134
Radiation 161
Ragwort 50
Rapunzel 55
Raths 17
Rebirth 141
Red deer, milk of 26
Reed 45
Religions 144
Rev. John Brand 130
Rheumatism 32
Rig-Veda 164, 167
Robin Goodfellow 148
Rollright Stones 160
Romans 54, 68, 71, 144
Round-eye 166
Rowan 38, 53

Rubus fructicosus 56
Rusalka 136
Rusalky 117, 147

Salamander 159
Salmon 73
Salvanelli 144
Sambucus nigra 44
Samhain 117, 119, 152-153
Sankchinnis 144
Satan 130
Satyrs 136, 148
Scissors 37
Scythe 37
Sea fairies 155
Selkies 145
Senecio jacobaea 50
Serpent 93, 99
Shade-foots 166
Shadow 32
Shakespeare 48, 71, 89
Shaman 164, 166
Shamantin 147
Shedim 159
Sherlock Holmes 127
Shoneys 155
Siddhi 3
Sidhe 3, 69
Silphe 159
Silverweed 26, 50
Sinend 48
Sir Arthur Conan Doyle 127
Sirens 145
Sithbheire 76
Sithean Beinne Bhoidhich 102
Sithein 18
Sjofn 155
Skosrâ 148
Skuld 155

Sle of Glass 23
Sleeping Beauty 55
Sloe 55
Snail 67
Solstices 152
Soma 167
Sorbus aucuparia 53
Sorcha 22
Soul 144
Souls 139
Spinning 108
Spinning wheel 36, 155
Spor sith 30
Spriggans 138
St Brigit 154
St Levan 18
St Patrick 23
St. John's wort 40
Stewart, John 122
Stone Age flints 134
Sun 138, 140
Sun god 166
Swan 99

Tam Lin 99, 168
Tarmach-de 60
Tempest, The 71
Teutons 144
Theosophical Society 149
Theseus 156
Thomas the Rhymer 57, 100, 168
Three Fates 155
Three Norns 155
Thymus vulgaris 48
Tiddy Mun 145
Tir Nan Og 22
Tolman 18
Toradh 27
Trifolium sp 52

Triple Goddess 52
Triple Moon Goddess 156
Trooping Fairies 9
Trousers 37
Trows 120
Tryamour 89
Tuatha de Danaan 9, 69, 131,
    152, 154-155, 166
Tuberculosis 32
Tudor of Llangollen 104
Twelfth Night 120
Tylwyth Teg 3, 84, 155

Uffington Horse 69
UFOs 161
Underworld 138, 156, 167
Undines 145, 159
Unseelie Court 119, 138, 152
Uranium 161
Urd 155
Urine 42

Vanadevatas 144
Vegetation spirits 148
Venus 68
Verdani 155
Vernal Equinox 117
Vile 144
Vivienne 146

Walsh, James 122
Washer at the Ford 152
Water 42, 158
Water fairies 111, 145
Weather 148
Weaver Goddess 155
Weaving 108
Wednesday 116
White ladies 147
Wild Hunt 67, 120
Wild thyme 48
Wildmen 136
Will o'the wisps 159
Wind Knots 148
Winter Hag 117
Winter Solstice 120
Witch 55, 122
Woden 67, 153
Wood woses 136, 148
Wood-wife 54, 144
Woodpecker 73
World Tree 168
Wright, Elsie 127

Y Fuwch Frech 62
Yeats, WB. 76, 127
Ynis Gwydrin 23
Yule 120, 122, 153
Yumboes 126

'The Spirits of ....' Series

"This really is a wonderful series of books.." Touchstone

Spirits of the Earth by Jaq D Hawkins

"It's all in here...really wonderful and useful stuff...I really couldn't put this excellent book down. I would thoroughly recommend this book" Touchstone

"A delight to read..a very highly informative and very readable book." Eastern Spirit

This is the first volume in the Spirits of the Earth series in which Jaq D Hawkins shares an understanding of the basic nature of elemental spirits with her readers. Within each volume,

Ms. Hawkins explains to us the nature of the element, types of spirits associated with each element, and correspondences in magical thought as well as rituals and divination methods in natural magic. Included in *Spirits of the Earth* are the types of natural objects, and sometimes man-made objects, which attract Earth Spirit inhabitants as well as methods to see or communicate with these elemental spirits, places of worship or invocation, and the nature of thought form spirits associated with the Earth element. From fanciful fairies to guardian spirits of stone circles, Spirits of the Earth is a 'must have' for anyone who has an interest in elemental spirits. ISBN 186163 002 6   £8.95

Spirits of the Air by Jaq D Hawkins

"will certainly appeal to all those interested in Paganism and folklore" Prediction

In this second volume in the Spirits of Earth series, Ms. Hawkins progresses into the inspirational realm of Air elemental spirits and continues to relate these spirits to magical correspondences, rituals and divination methods. Included in Spirits of the Air are examples of types of Air spirits, methods for communicating and seeking cooperation from these spirits, expanded instructions for dealing with thought-form spirits and more. From spirits of storms to messengers of the gods themselves, Spirits of the Air is an integral sourcebook for seekers of elemental magic. ISBN 186163 0654 £8.95

Spirits of the Fire by Jaq D Hawkins

In this third volume of the Spirits of the Elements Series, we encounter yet a new perspective of elemental spirits - and find ourselves confronted with all of the passion and intensity, and even the dangers, of the element of Fire. Included in Spirits of the Fire are new aspects of the nature and types of elemental spirits as well as new approaches to elemental spirit magic. Also included are methods for focusing and directing the dynamic forces of Fire spirits, and for evoking the power of the spirit of Fire through ecstatic dance and other methods. Whether we seek the assistance of a spirit of a flame or the potency of the spirit of passion in magic, Spirits of the Fire is an essential addition to the library of any practitioner of elemental spirit magic. ISBN 186163 076 X   **£8.95**

'Spirtis of the Aether' in Preparation

FREE DETAILED CATALOGUE

Capall Bann is owned and run by people actively involved in many of the areas in which we publish. A detailed illustrated catalogue is available on request, SAE or International Postal Coupon appreciated. **Titles can be ordered direct from Capall Bann, post free in the UK** (cheque or PO with order) or from good bookshops and specialist outlets.

Do contact us for details on the latest releases at: **Capall Bann Publishing, Freshfields, Chieveley, Berks, RG20 8TF.** Titles include:

A Breath Behind Time, Terri Hector
Angels and Goddesses - Celtic Christianity & Paganism, M. Howard
Arthur - The Legend Unveiled, C Johnson & E Lung
Astrology The Inner Eye - A Guide in Everyday Language, E Smith
Auguries and Omens - The Magical Lore of Birds, Yvonne Aburrow
Asyniur - Womens Mysteries in the Northern Tradition, S McGrath
Beginnings - Geomancy, Builder's Rites & Electional Astrology in the
    European Tradition, Nigel Pennick
Between Earth and Sky, Julia Day
Book of the Veil , Peter Paddon
Caer Sidhe - Celtic Astrology and Astronomy, Vol 1, Michael Bayley
Caer Sidhe - Celtic Astrology and Astronomy, Vol 2 M Bayley
Call of the Horned Piper, Nigel Jackson
Cat's Company, Ann Walker
Celtic Faery Shamanism, Catrin James
Celtic Faery Shamanism - The Wisdom of the Otherworld, Catrin James
Celtic Lore & Druidic Ritual, Rhiannon Ryall
Celtic Sacrifice - Pre Christian Ritual & Religion, Marion Pearce
Celtic Saints and the Glastonbury Zodiac, Mary Caine
Circle and the Square, Jack Gale
Compleat Vampyre - The Vampyre Shaman, Nigel Jackson
Creating Form From the Mist - The Wisdom of Women in Celtic Myth and
    Culture, Lynne Sinclair-Wood
Crystal Clear - A Guide to Quartz Crystal, Jennifer Dent
Crystal Doorways, Simon & Sue Lilly
Crossing the Borderlines - Guising, Masking & Ritual Animal Disguise in the
    European Tradition, Nigel Pennick
Dragons of the West, Nigel Pennick
Earth Dance - A Year of Pagan Rituals, Jan Brodie
Earth Harmony - Places of Power, Holiness & Healing, Nigel Pennick
Earth Magic, Margaret McArthur

Eildon Tree (The) Romany Language & Lore, Michael Hoadley
Enchanted Forest - The Magical Lore of Trees, Yvonne Aburrow
Eternal Priestess, Sage Weston
Eternally Yours Faithfully, Roy Radford & Evelyn Gregory
Everything You Always Wanted To Know About Your Body, But So Far
    Nobody's Been Able To Tell You, Chris Thomas & D Baker
Face of the Deep - Healing Body & Soul, Penny Allen
Fairies in the Irish Tradition, Molly Gowen
Familiars - Animal Powers of Britain, Anna Franklin
Fool's First Steps, (The) Chris Thomas
Forest Paths - Tree Divination, Brian Harrison, Ill. S. Rouse
From Past to Future Life, Dr Roger Webber
Gardening For Wildlife Ron Wilson
God Year, The, Nigel Pennick & Helen Field
Goddess on the Cross, Dr George Young
Goddess Year, The, Nigel Pennick & Helen Field
Goddesses, Guardians & Groves, Jack Gale
Handbook For Pagan Healers, Liz Joan
Handbook of Fairies, Ronan Coghlan
Healing Book, The, Chris Thomas and Diane Baker
Healing Homes, Jennifer Dent
Healing Journeys, Paul Williamson
Healing Stones, Sue Philips
Herb Craft - Shamanic & Ritual Use of Herbs, Lavender & Franklin
Hidden Heritage - Exploring Ancient Essex, Terry Johnson
Hub of the Wheel, Skytoucher
In Search of Herne the Hunter, Eric Fitch
Inner Celtia, Alan Richardson & David Annwn
Inner Mysteries of the Goths, Nigel Pennick
Inner Space Workbook - Develop Thru Tarot, C Summers & J Vayne
Intuitive Journey, Ann Walker Isis - African Queen, Akkadia Ford
Journey Home, The, Chris Thomas
Kecks, Keddles & Kesh - Celtic Lang & The Cog Almanac, Bayley
Language of the Psycards, Berenice
Legend of Robin Hood, The, Richard Rutherford-Moore
Lid Off the Cauldron, Patricia Crowther
Light From the Shadows - Modern Traditional Witchcraft, Gwyn
Living Tarot, Ann Walker
Lore of the Sacred Horse, Marion Davies
Lost Lands & Sunken Cities (2nd ed.), Nigel Pennick
Magic of Herbs - A Complete Home Herbal, Rhiannon Ryall
Magical Guardians - Exploring the Spirit and Nature of Trees, Philip Heselton
Magical History of the Horse, Janet Farrar & Virginia Russell
Magical Lore of Animals, Yvonne Aburrow
Magical Lore of Cats, Marion Davies
Magical Lore of Herbs, Marion Davies

Magick Without Peers, Ariadne Rainbird & David Rankine
Masks of Misrule - Horned God & His Cult in Europe, Nigel Jackson
Medicine For The Coming Age, Lisa Sand MD
Medium Rare - Reminiscences of a Clairvoyant, Muriel Renard
Menopausal Woman on the Run, Jaki da Costa
Mind Massage - 60 Creative Visualisations, Marlene Maundrill
Mirrors of Magic - Evoking the Spirit of the Dewponds, P Heselton
Moon Mysteries, Jan Brodie
Mysteries of the Runes, Michael Howard
Mystic Life of Animals, Ann Walker
New Celtic Oracle The, Nigel Pennick & Nigel Jackson
Oracle of Geomancy, Nigel Pennick
Pagan Feasts - Seasonal Food for the 8 Festivals, Franklin & Phillips
Patchwork of Magic - Living in a Pagan World, Julia Day
Pathworking - A Practical Book of Guided Meditations, Pete Jennings
Personal Power, Anna Franklin
Pickingill Papers - The Origins of Gardnerian Wicca, Bill Liddell
Pillars of Tubal Cain, Nigel Jackson
Places of Pilgrimage and Healing, Adrian Cooper
Practical Divining, Richard Foord
Practical Meditation, Steve Hounsome
Practical Spirituality, Steve Hounsome
Psychic Self Defence - Real Solutions, Jan Brodie
Real Fairies, David Tame
Reality - How It Works & Why It Mostly Doesn't, Rik Dent
Romany Tapestry, Michael Houghton
Runic Astrology, Nigel Pennick
Sacred Animals, Gordon MacLellan
Sacred Celtic Animals, Marion Davies, Ill. Simon Rouse
Sacred Dorset - On the Path of the Dragon, Peter Knight
Sacred Grove - The Mysteries of the Forest, Yvonne Aburrow
Sacred Geometry, Nigel Pennick
Sacred Nature, Ancient Wisdom & Modern Meanings, A Cooper
Sacred Ring - Pagan Origins of British Folk Festivals, M. Howard
Season of Sorcery - On Becoming a Wisewoman, Poppy Palin
Seasonal Magic - Diary of a Village Witch, Paddy Slade
Secret Places of the Goddess, Philip Heselton
Secret Signs & Sigils, Nigel Pennick
Self Enlightenment, Mayan O'Brien
Spirits of the Air, Jaq D Hawkins
Spirits of the Earth, Jaq D Hawkins
Spirits of the Earth, Jaq D Hawkins
Stony Gaze, Investigating Celtic Heads John Billingsley
Stumbling Through the Undergrowth , Mark Kirwan-Heyhoe
Subterranean Kingdom, The, revised 2nd ed, Nigel Pennick
Symbols of Ancient Gods, Rhiannon Ryall

Talking to the Earth, Gordon MacLellan
Taming the Wolf - Full Moon Meditations, Steve Hounsome
Teachings of the Wisewomen, Rhiannon Ryall
The Other Kingdoms Speak, Helena Hawley
Tree: Essence of Healing, Simon & Sue Lilly
Tree: Essence, Spirit & Teacher, Simon & Sue Lilly
Through the Veil, Peter Paddon
Torch and the Spear, Patrick Regan
Understanding Chaos Magic, Jaq D Hawkins
Vortex - The End of History, Mary Russell
Warp and Weft - In Search of the I-Ching, William de Fancourt
Warriors at the Edge of Time, Jan Fry
Water Witches, Tony Steele
Way of the Magus, Michael Howard
Weaving a Web of Magic, Rhiannon Ryall
West Country Wicca, Rhiannon Ryall
Wildwitch - The Craft of the Natural Psychic, Poppy Palin
Wildwood King , Philip Kane
Witches of Oz, Matthew & Julia Philips
Wondrous Land - The Faery Faith of Ireland by Dr Kay Mullin
Working With the Merlin, Geoff Hughes
Your Talking Pet, Ann Walker

FREE detailed catalogue and
FREE 'Inspiration' magazine

Contact: Capall Bann Publishing, Freshfields, Chieveley, Berks, RG20 8TF